M/

What
Every Woman
Should Know
...About Her Car

Illustrated by Linda Wisenauer

What Every Woman Should Know ...About Her Car

Dorothy Jackson

CHILTON BOOK COMPANY
Radnor, Pennsylvania

Copyright © 1974 by Dorothy Jackson
First Edition   All Rights Reserved
Published in Radnor, Pa. by Chilton Book Company
and simultaneously in Ontario, Canada by
Thomas Nelson & Sons Ltd.

Designed by Carole L. DeCrescenzo

Manufactured in the United States of America

Library of Congress Cataloging in Publication Data

Jackson, Dorothy.
   What every woman should know . . . about her car

   1. Automobiles—Popular works.   2. Automobiles—
Maintenance and repair.   I. Title.
TL146.5.J32 1974   629.22'22'024042   74-17326
ISBN 0-8019-6000-2
ISBN 0-8019-6001-0 (pbk)

Foreword

This book is intended to help people, mainly women, who know little or nothing about their car. It is not my intention to ridicule or make fun of your inexperience. Rather, I will tell you plainly and simply some things that can save you a lot of trouble on the road, increase your knowledge of your automobile and make it easier for you to explain problems to your mechanic.

Dorothy Jackson

Acknowledgments

I am deeply indebted to Mr. Charles Yarnall, my employer and friend, for the help and knowledge he has given me over the years. I would not have even attempted this book without his encouragement.

For assistance with researching certain chapters and sections of this book, I wish to give particular thanks to Mr. Robert Beling, Vice President of the Fred S. James Insurance Co., Mr. Sig Overgaard of the Nationwide Insurance Co., and Carlson's Body Shop of West Chester, Pa.

I wish to thank special friends such as Mr. and Mrs. G. H. Sulzer and Mrs. Sidney Rabin who gave me little boosts and the incentive to go ahead and write this book. In addition, State Trooper Duchemin was responsible for gently pushing me to take the State Inspection Examination.

Finally, I would like to thank the Chilton Book Company for giving me the opportunity to provide this book for all women who must come to terms with the automobile.

Contents

INTRODUCTION   1

GLOSSARY OF AUTOMOTIVE TERMS   7

Chapter 1   YOUR CAR   33

Chapter 2   PLAY IT SAFE   53

Chapter 3   ON THE ROAD   63

Chapter 4   WHAT'S THAT THING?   89

Chapter 5   WHAT YOU CAN CHECK YOURSELF   123

Chapter 6   IF IT WON'T START   145

Chapter 7   FIX IT YOURSELF   158

Chapter 8   WATCH OUT FOR THE RIPOFF   180

INDEX   195

What
Every Woman
Should Know
...About Her Car

Introduction

My reason for writing this book for women is twofold. I know that 56% of the drivers in the United States are male. This means that all the rest are . . . right, just like you and me. Almost half the drivers in the country are female, yet most auto manuals are aimed

exclusively at a male audience, certainly people who have a good working knowledge of autos, tools and complex machinery. After all, how many women have been brought up on a steady diet of nuts and bolts or carburetors and alternators?

With male chauvinism dying hard and women's liberation flourishing, isn't it high time we women learned something for ourselves about the automobile? So many people, especially women, show their limited automotive knowledge and are therefore easy prey for the garage or gas station that wants to take advantage of them.

I have worked for thirty-one years in an independent garage and have learned a lot about cars and something about men and

Those days of chivalrous knights are gone so today's woman has to fend for herself.

women. I have heard both sexes come into our garage and say: "I just don't know a thing about cars and I don't care as long as it runs." This is fine except these people are the ones who scream the loudest when they get their repair bill. By taking this "don't bother me" attitude, such people are inviting the unethical garage to take them over the coals.

Don't be like the female who came to our garage and said: "My car isn't running smoothly." Our mechanic said: "Sounds like one of your plugs is missing." She replied: "I don't remember losing it."

Had she known some of the mechanic's jargon, she might have realized that he was talking about a spark plug that was misfiring, not missing from the engine.

So let's get with it and see if we can learn some of the mysteries of the automobile.

A car is nothing more than a piece of machinery. It was not born and it cannot talk although in a way it communicates with you by making noises as a warning that it is not well. After reading this book, you will be able to interpret these noises and determine how serious your car's problem is.

Today's woman knows how to start a lawn mower, fiddle with the washing machine and fix the fuses that blow out; so why can't she master the automobile? There is no reason why she can't, in my opinion. You don't have to learn how to overhaul the car but you can learn what parts are what, where they are and what they do. Remember, a car is a machine and the part that works today may fail tomorrow, just like parts of our own bodies. But also like our own bodies, a common sense approach to taking care of it can prevent failure.

When and How to Use this Book

This book is divided into eight chapters which I feel cover most situations and problems that might arise with your car. In addition *What Every Woman Should Know ... About Her Car* will provide you with a good orientation to the automobile, a field previously dominated by men.

Consult this book either before you buy or operate your car, since, as with any other piece of machinery, problems will arise. When you have any difficulties, read the part of this book that relates to that specific problem. Using *What Every Woman Should Know ... About Her Car* this way can save you time, money and aggravation. I have written the text as simply as possible, and I hope that it is easy to understand. Anyone, after reading this book and without prior knowledge of mechanics, can intelligently discuss her car's problem with a mechanic. Ladies, if you can read a recipe book and follow the instructions, you can follow this book

and profit from it. You know that in most men's estimation the woman driver is the low one on the totem pole. We know this isn't necessarily so and by quietly learning the subject we can then carry our own weight.

In my opinion, woman drivers are more cautious for the simple reason that men are more often in a hurry and high-tempered. They take more chances than women and, of course, are supposed to be quite brave. A woman who owns a car should be looked at and judged on the same basis as a man who owns a car. She should and can be just as good a driver and know just as much as the average man about a car—he doesn't know everything either.

Strength isn't a factor in driving; any woman can keep a car clean, diagnose its ills, talk to a mechanic and know the law concerning licenses, inspections and insurance. She should receive all respect due a car owner and operator and she should assume the attendant responsibilities.

Try doing without your car for a day or two, and you will see how important it is. You can walk the kids to school, walk to the stores or walk to work . . . well, you know what it would be like.

When the happy day comes to buy a new car, a woman should be able to handle the purchase herself and know the procedure for assuming the title, understanding prices and financing and paying interest and sales taxes—all without having to depend on

Girls, let's get to know the car.

anyone else, especially a man! We are told that a lot of the cars sold are purchased because the woman buyer thinks the colors are pretty or because they go well with her hair or eyes. Perhaps that does happen, but it might well be 99% myth. However, is any of this as important as economy, performance, what you can afford, safety and reliability?

Glossary of
Automotive Terms

ACCELERATION   The force or pressure against resistance; an increase in the speed of an automobile.

ACCELERATOR   The gas pedal with which you control the speed of the engine.

ACCELERATOR PUMP   A device within the carburetor which can give a rapid supply of gasoline to the cylinders.

ACCESSORIES   The optional extras for your car; i.e., radio, heater, power brakes.

ACID   The electrolyte in the battery is commonly called battery acid.

ADVANCE   Moving forward the timing with which the spark plugs fire.

AERIAL   The radio antenna.

AIR CLEANER (or Air Filter)   The device on the top of the engine which cleans or filters the outside air before it goes into the carburetor to mix with gasoline.

AIR CONDITIONING   A device run by the car's engine which cools incoming air and then pumps it throughout the inside of the car.

AIR-COOLED ENGINE   Although most automotive engines are cooled by water from the radiator, a few (mainly Volkswagens) are cooled by outside air drawn in by a cooling fan and forced over the outsides of the cylinders.

AIR/FUEL RATIO   The ratio of outside air and gasoline which is mixed by the carburetor and then sent to the cylinders to be burned.

AIR PUMP   A component of the emission control systems on some cars which pumps fresh air to join with unburned hydrocarbons and be burned in the exhaust manifold.

ALIGNMENT   A job which is done on the front suspension and steering system in order to keep it pointing straight ahead and keep both front wheels in the proper relationship to each other and to the road.

ALTERNATOR   A device which is turned by the engine and generates electricity to recharge the battery.

AMMETER   A meter which measures the rate of current flow through a circuit and shows it on the dashboard gauge.

AMPERES (Amps)   The units which current flow is measured in.

ANALYZER   Large electronic equipment which diagnostic centers and big repair garages use to monitor an "analyze" the systems of an automobile engine.

ANTIFREEZE   A petroleum- or alcohol-based liquid which is added to the water in a car's radiator to keep it from freezing in the winter and boiling over in hot weather.

ARMATURE   Parts contained in generators, starters and regulators; they are moved by magnetic attraction.

ATF (Automatic Transmission Fluid)   A low viscosity, high detergent oil-based liquid used to lubricate the internal parts of a transmission and able to withstand high temperatures. This fluid can also be used in the power steering pump.

AUTOMATIC TRANSMISSION   A device which transfers the power produced by the engine to the rear wheels and also gives the driver control over the engine's power for various situations (passing, cruising, accelerating). These tasks are performed without the driver having to use a clutch and gear shift, i.e., automatically.

AXLE   In its most simple form, an axle is something around which a wheel turns. However, automobiles use two specialized types of axles: a rear axle which is also a drive axle and a front axle which can also be steered to the right or left.

BACKFIRE   A loud popping noise most often the result of a poorly tuned engine. When the ignition timing is off by too much, combusion can occur halfway out of the cylinder or even all the way out in the exhaust manifold.

BACKING PLATE   The ends of the axles on which are mounted the brake linings and wheel cylinders. The brake drum is then mounted over this assembly and the wheel is bolted to the outside of the drum.

BACKUP LIGHTS   The white lights at the rear of the car which come on when the gear selector is placed in Reverse. They indicate to anyone behind that you are backing-up and they also light up the area so you can see where you are backing.

BAKELITE   A very hard, black rubber-like material used for some automotive parts: ex. the distributor cap.

BALANCING   The process of distributing the weight on the circumference of the wheels so that they spin evenly on the axle.

BARREL   The main fuel passage in the carburetor. This will usually be seen as a one barrel, a two barrel, or a four barrel carburetor.

BATTERY   The current produced by the alternator is stored in the battery and then doled out to the various electrical components while constantly being recharged by the alternator.

BATTERY ACID   The liquid inside each battery cell whose technical name is electrolyte. When you add plain water to the battery, the reaction inside produces electrolyte.

BATTERY BOOSTER   The battery that is used to jump start a dead battery.

BATTERY CABLES   The cables or large wires which attach to each end of the battery. One is positive and carries current to the engine electrical system and the other cable is negative and grounds the system.

BATTERY CELLS   The places under each battery cap where electrolyte is stored.

BATTERY CHARGING   The process of replacing the electricity that the engine draws from the battery. Replacement or recharging is done by the alternator.

BATTERY TERMINALS (or Posts)   The short metal studs which come out of each end of the top of the battery and to which the battery cables are attached.

BEARINGS   A wear-resistant metal support for a turning shaft; i.e., crankshaft and camshaft bearings.

BELTED   A method of tire construction characterized by circumferential plies.

BIAS-PLY   Another method of tire construction, this one characterized by crisscrossing plies.

BLEEDING   The process of draining and refilling the hydraulic brake system with brake fluid so as to eliminate air bubbles within the system.

BLOCK   The heavy, cast iron, basic part of the engine before internal and external engine parts are added.

BLOW-BY   Combustion and vapor leakage past the piston rings and into the crankcase causing loss of power.

BLOWER MOTOR   An electrical motor which blows hot air out of the heater and into the passenger compartment of the car.

BODY   The external, enclosing part of the car: roof, fenders, doors, hood, trunk.

BOLTS   When speaking of nuts and bolts, the bolt is the part with threads on its *outside* which the nut screws onto or over.

BORE AND STROKE   Bore is the diameter of one engine cylinder given in inches; the stroke is the distance one piston travels— also given in inches. These figures are often seen together, ex. 3.680 x 3.130 in.

BRAKES   The system and its components used to stop the car.

Disc Brakes   An advanced brake system using pinching pads instead of expanding shoes.

Drum Brakes   The standard brake system which uses shoes that expand and rub against a drum.

Brake Fluid   The hydraulic fluid used to maintain pressure in either a disc or drum brake system.

Hand Brake   The parking brake, whether it is applied by hand or foot.

Brake Lines   The conductor tubing system which contains and carries brake fluid throughout the system.

Brake Lights   When the brake pedal is pressed, the taillights (or brake lights) are switched on to warn following cars that you are stopping.

Power Brakes   Either a disc or drum brake system with power assistance to brake pedal application.

Self-adjusting Brakes   On many new cars the brakes will keep themselves in adjustment by resetting themselves when you back up and apply the brakes.

BREAKER POINTS   The "points" discussed in the "Ignition" section of this book. They are located under the distributor cap, they direct the electrical current coming from the coil, and they are always replaced during a tune-up.

BREAK-IN   Gradually wearing-in or acclimating a new engine to running conditions.

BREATHER   A vent on the valve cover which allows fumes to escape from the crankcase. On older cars these fumes escaped right into the atmosphere; on newer cars they are recirculated and burned in the engine. In either case, they still exit through a breather.

BUCKET SEATS   Individual passenger seats are called bucket seats because they conform to or surround the body more than flat or "bench" seats.

BUMPERS   The heavy chrome pieces on the extreme front and rear of a car which protect the rest of the car and absorb shocks in an accident.

BUSHINGS   Very similar to a bearing though usually applied to smaller shafts.

CABLE   A heavily insulated wire such as a battery cable or a spark plug cable.

CAMBER   A term used to describe front-end design and alignment. Camber refers to the outward tilt of the tops of the front wheels. They do this so that when the car is loaded and moving forward, the natural tendency to tilt inward will cause them to become correctly vertical.

CAMSHAFT   As the crankshaft turns inside the engine, a heavy chain attached to it turns another, smaller shaft which opens and closes the intake and exhaust valves. This shaft is the camshaft.

CANCER   Rust that eats away at the body from the inside out.

CAPACITY   The maximum amount of liquid held by a container or system. Ex. oil pan capacity, transmission fluid capacity, fuel tank capacity.

CARBON   A by-product of combustion which will eventually build up inside an engine.

CARBON MONOXIDE   A poisonous, gaseous by-product of combustion.

CARBURETOR   A device which meters and mixes gasoline to the proper proportion with air to be burned in the cylinders of an engine.

CASTER   Another term used to describe front end design and alignment. Caster refers to a slight backward tilt of the center axis of the front wheels—much like a caster on furniture legs.

CHASSIS   The automobile frame with the engine and all running parts in place but minus the body, interior, trim, and accessories.

CHATTER   A noise heard from the clutch on standard transmission cars. The presence of a chatter usually indicates a bad clutch bearing.

CHOKE   A system (either manual or automatic) which richens the air/fuel mixture in the carburetor to make a cold engine run smoother.

CIRCUIT   The course that an electrical current follows from its origin to the final source (such as a bulb) or to ground.

CLEARANCE   The tiny space separating two moving parts, usually coated with oil. Ex. the space between the piston and cylinder wall.

CLUTCH   A mechanical or hydraulic device which momentarily disconnects the spinning engine from the transmission gears and shafts so that gears can be changed or shifted.

COIL   An electrical device which receives power from the battery and, like a transformer, steps the current up to a higher voltage to go through the distributor and fire the spark plugs.

COMBUSTION   A burning or explosion within the cylinder caused by igniting a gaseous vapor with a spark.

COMBUSTION CHAMBER   The cylinder or the top of the cylinder where combustion occurs.

COMPONENTS   The parts that make up a system. Ex. The gas tank, fuel lines, fuel pump, fuel filter and carburetor make up the fuel system.

COMPRESSION   As the piston moves upward in the cylinder, it "compresses" the air/fuel mixture in the top of the cylinder where it is then ignited by the spark plug. The compression ratio is the amount by which compression of the air/fuel mixture diminishes its area.

COMPRESSION GAUGE   A measuring device which is inserted into the spark plug hole. When the engine is turned over, compression occurs but there is no spark plug to ignite the mixture. At this point the gauge measures the amount of compression which is a good indicator of the condition of the pistons, cylinder walls and piston rings.

COMPRESSOR   A component of the automotive air conditioning system that condenses the gas (freon) in the system.

CONDENSATION   The changing of a gas vapor to a liquid by cooling, i.e., steam to water.

CONDENSER   A component of the ignition system (in the distributor) which prevents the arcing of electrical current across the contact surfaces of the points.

CONDUCTOR   This name is usually used when discussing electricity and means material capable of carrying electricity with minimum loss, such as copper wire.

CONNECTING ROD   The device which connects the piston to the crankshaft. It is designed and attached so that it can rotate around the crankshaft when the piston forces it down.

CONSOLE   The decorative and functional box between bucket seats.

COOLANT   The water and antifreeze mixture in the cooling system of an engine which picks up heat from the engine and in turn cools the engine.

COOLING SYSTEM   The process by which the coolant in the radiator is cooled by incoming air and then goes through the engine to cool it and also carry off the heat the engine produces. The components involved in this process: radiator, hoses, fan, water pump, thermostat and water jackets.

CORNERING   The handling ability of a car or its resistance to skidding and rolling when rounding a sharp curve.

CORROSION   The eating away of a substance, usually metal, by acids.

COTTER PIN   A piece of hard wire which is pushed through a hole in the end of a bolt *after* the nut is screwed on and then bent open so that even if the nut uncrews, it cannot come off. This is mainly a safety device used on wheels, steering and suspension systems.

CRANKCASE   The bottom part of the engine where the crankshaft is housed. On older engines this was a separate part but modern blocks are all one piece.

CRANKING OR STARTING   Turning the engine over with the starter motor via the ignition key.

CRANKSHAFT   A heavy shaft at the bottom of the engine which turns the piston power into turning power and transmits it to the transmission.

CUPPING   Depressions or cup-shaped wear patterns on a tire.

CURRENT   The movement of electricity through wires or through a whole circuit.

CYCLE   A series of events such as the "four stroke cycle" in an engine which consists of the intake stroke, the compression stroke, the power stroke and the exhaust stroke of the pistons.

CYLINDER(S)   The chamber or hole in the engine block where the piston fits and in which the piston travels up and down. The number of these chambers in a given engine, i.e., a four, six or eight cylinder engine.

CYLINDER HEAD   The engine component which provides a cover for the cylinders and which, on some engines, houses the spark plugs and valves.

DASHBOARD   The front part of the passenger compartment, located under the windshield which contains the instrument cluster, radio, glove compartment, etc.

DEFROSTER   One of the parts of the heating system which blows air onto the inside of the windshield to eliminate steamed-up windows.

DETONATION   Burning of the air/fuel mixture in the combustion chamber which occurs too early and causes a knocking sound.

DIAGNOSE (Troubleshooting)   Assessing the symptons of an automotive problem and locating the source of that problem.

DIESEL ENGINE   An internal combustion engine which does not use spark plugs to ignite fuel in the chamber; used most often in trucks.

DIESELING   Ignition which occurs too late is called postignition or dieseling. When you shut the car off and it continues to run, this is called dieseling.

DIFFERENTIAL   The center of the rear axle in which is a gear arrangement that allows the two rear wheels to run at different speeds.

DIMMER   The floor switch in a car which lets you switch from low to high headlight beams.

DIPSTICK   This is the stick used to measure the amount of oil in the engine's oil system; there is a similar one to measure the amount of fluid in an automatic transmission.

DIRECT CURRENT (DC)   Electrical current which flows in one direction only.

DISCHARGE   The departure of current from the battery.

DISPLACEMENT   The volume of all the cylinders in an engine added together and expressed in cubic inches, i.e., a 351 cu. in. engine.

DISTRIBUTOR   The ignition system device which parcels out the high voltage current from the coil to the spark plugs.

Distributor Cap   The black bakelite top of the distributor from which the spark plug cables emerge.

Distributor Cables   The heavy wires which conduct high voltage current from the coil to the spark plugs via the distributor. Also called spark plug cable.

Distributor Rotor   The uppermost internal part of the distributor which directs the high voltage coil current to the proper spark plug cable.

DRIVESHAFT   A long shaft which is turned by the transmission and in turn transmits that turning power to the rear axle and rear wheels.

DRUM   See "Brakes."

DWELL ANGLE   The number of degrees which the distributor shaft rotates between openings of the points.

DWELL METER   A gauge designed to measure the dwell angle to properly tune the ignition system.

ELECTRICAL SYSTEM   That automotive system which originates, stores, disperses and utilizes electricity necessary to run the engine and accessories. Components include the battery, alternator, starter, ignition switch (key), regulator, coil, distributor, spark plugs and all the wires, cables and terminals required to connect and control these components.

ELECTRODE   Two terminals in an electrical system that are separated by a gap which the current must jump, i.e., the electrode tip of a spark plug.

ELECTROLYTE   The liquid inside an automotive battery which is composed of about 60% water and 40% sulphuric acid.

EMISSION CONTROL SYSTEMS   The added-on components or internal engine designs which come on newer cars and reduce the pollutants caused by operating the engine.

ENGINE   The source of power in an automobile; the creation of this power being by internal combustion: the burning of air and fuel in a closed cylinder whose expansion rotates a shaft.

ENGINE MOUNTS   The legs of the engine. The rubber and steel parts of the engine which hold it in place yet give it slight flexibility.

ETHYL GASOLINE   A chemical added to gasoline to eliminate knocking.

EVAPORATION   The process of fluid turning into a vapor either from heat or exposure to air.

EXHAUST   The by-product or leftovers from the combustion process which is expelled from the engine.

EXHAUST MANIFOLD   The cast iron tubes in which the exhaust is expelled and which collect into one pipe, the exhaust pipe, to travel to the rear of the car via a noise muffler and then into the atmosphere.

FADING   When brakes are applied constantly or too frequently as in descending a hill, the shoes and drum or the disc and caliper become unusually hot and their abrasive or stopping ability fades. This can be extremely dangerous as braking ability can be reduced by 50%.

FAN   A bladed device which is turned by the engine and thereby draws cool air in through the radiator to cool the water in the cooling system.

FAN BELTS   The rubber belt connection by which the engine turns the fan. Also often used to describe any drive belt turned by the engine such as the power steering belt or the air-conditioning belt.

FATIGUE   Metal collapse due to heavy stress and/or long wear.

FEATHERING   Uneven wearing of the inner and outer edges of a tire.

FEELER GAUGE   A tool with separate blades or wires of exact thicknesses used to measure the size of a gap between two surfaces such as the gap between the points and the gap between the center and lower electrodes of a spark plug.

FIREWALL   The metal wall or panel that separates the engine compartment from the passenger compartment.

FIRING ORDER   The sequence in which the spark plugs fire as determined by the timing of the distributor.

FISHTAIL   The breaking loose or skidding of the rear wheels due to an oversupply of power, particularly while going too fast around a corner.

FLASHERS   The simultaneous blinking of the turn signals for safety and warning purposes.

FLOAT BOWL   A small holding tank in the carburetor where the fuel supply is stored briefly before being mixed with air and sent to the engine.

FLOODING   Pumping the gas pedal so much while trying to start the car that the intake manifold and cylinder become filled with raw gas and too wet to start.

FLOORBOARD   Mainly an older automotive term, this refers to the floor of the passenger compartment.

FLUID   Really any liquid but in automotive jargan this refers specifically to brake fluid and automatic transmission fluid.

FOULING   This is what happens to spark plugs when they have been in the engine for too long or when the rings are worn. It is a build-up of carbon and oily deposits on the electrodes.

FRAME   The heavy steel skeleton of the car which the engine is mounted into and the body is bolted onto.

FREON   The gas which the air-conditioning system uses to cool the air.

FRICTION   The resistance to movement caused by two parts rubbing against each other. This principle is used in the brake system where the shoes rub against the drum and friction causes the drum to stop turning. There is also friction inside the engine where the piston rubs up and down against the walls of the cylinder but extra smooth surfaces and the presence of oil between these surfaces minimizes friction so the parts won't wear out or stop like the brake drum.

FRONT SUSPENSION   The attachment of the front wheels and steering system to the car frame by springs and struts.

FUEL   Any material that produces heat or power by burning. Gasoline or diesel fuel are the most common fuels for internal combustion engines.

FUEL INJECTION   A sophisticated method of metering and mixing fuel with air and timing its injection into the cylinders. Fuel injection is a substitute or replacement for a carburetor but it is expensive and usually seen on high performance cars only.

FUEL NOZZLE   The main mixing jet in a carburetor.

FUEL PUMP   A mechanical or electrical device to bring gas from the tank to the carburetor under pressure.

FUEL SYSTEM   The process of providing fuel to be burned in the cylinders and the components of that system: fuel tank, fuel lines, fuel pump, fuel filter, carburetor and intake manifold.

FUEL TANK   The storage tank beneath the trunk of the car where fuel is held before being pumped to the carburetor.

FUMES   Gaseous vapors. Fumes to be concerned about are those which result from a fuel leak or an exhaust leak.

FUSE   A metal strip in a glass case which melts and breaks the electrical circuit if the current flow becomes too strong.

GASKET   Some soft, thin material (usually cork or copper) used to create a seal between two metal parts. When the two surfaces are tightened together with the gasket between them, it seals that junction from leakage.

GASOLINE   A highly flammable hydrocarbon, petroleum-based fuel used mainly as an automotive fuel.

GAUGES   Either a tool for measuring gaps, thicknesses and pressures or an instrument to measure and indicate quantities.

GEAR SHIFT   The lever inside the passenger compartment used to select and change transmission gears and speeds manually.

GEAR RATIO   The number of teeth on one gear compared to the number of teeth on a meshing gear. If a gear having ten teeth is meshed with a gear having thirty teeth, the gear ratio is one to three. So, if the smaller gear turns completely around once, the larger gear will be turned around one-third of a full rotation.

GENERATOR   This component can be found on older cars but it has been replaced by the alternator on newer cars. Its function, however, is the same: to produce electricity to be stored in the battery and to recharge it.

GRABBING   A problem in the automotive brake system characterized by the brakes overreacting to pedal pressure or pulling to either side when the pedal is applied.

GROUND   Although this concept may seem difficult and even illogical, think of a car's electrical circuit as beginning at the positive post of the battery. Then imagine all the wires, lights and other electrical components in the circuit strung out in a straight line to the very last component on the line, say, a taillight. The current starts at the battery and travels through all the other components until it goes through the taillight. But, as you will recall, electricity must travel a complete circuit in order to be useful. So if that last taillight is not reconnected to the battery somehow, there will be no complete circuit and electricity cannot flow at all. Rather than running another wire back to the battery, the car's frame is used to perform this return function. Because steel is a good conductor of electricity and because there is such a large mass of it in the frame, it provides a less complicated way to complete the circuit. If you are wondering why you do not get a shock by touching the car, remember that the battery only puts out 12 volts—not enough to shock. It is only in the coil that the 12 volt current is stepped up to 20,000 volts to fire the spark plugs.

HANDBRAKE   This is the emergency brake—whether it is operated by hand or foot.

HEADLIGHTS   These are the two or four lamps at the front of the car which light the way and this includes the high beams and their dimmer switch.

HEATER   This is the component inside the car through which hot water from the cooling system flows and is radiated to warm the passenger compartment.

HOOD   The part of the car's body which opens and closes to provide an access cover for the engine compartment.

HORN   An electrically operated noisemaker usually mounted behind the grille and operated at the steering wheel.

HORSEPOWER   Horsepower is the ability to do the work of one horse. A 200 horsepower engine can do the work of 200 horses.

HOSES   The rubber tubes in a car which carry either water in the cooling system, air in the vacuum system, fluid in a hydraulic system or freon in the air-conditioning system.

HYDRAULICS   Any process that uses the force or power of a compressed liquid to effect a mechanical reaction.

Hydraulic Brakes   The system in which brake fluid under pressure in a closed system is used to cause an expansion of the brake shoes against the drum.

Hydraulic Valves   The system within the engine whereby oil under pressure is used to open and close the fuel intake and exhaust outlet valves.

HYDROCARBONS   Hydrocarbons are really unburned gasoline. They are a result of either gasoline which was not completely burned in the combustion process or of the simple evaporation of liquid gasoline. So the fumes coming from an open gas can are hydrocarbons caused by fuel evaporation. Hydrocarbons are one of the three main pollutants caused by an automobile.

HYDROMETER   This is an instrument which determines the state of the battery charge by measuring the weight of the electrolyte compared to the weight of water.

IDLE   When the engine is running at its lowest speed above stalling but is disconnected from the drive train (by being in Neutral) so that its power is not being used for useful work.

IDLE ADJUSTMENT   Controlling the speed with a screw on the carburetor at which the engine idles.

IDLE LIMITER CAPS   Plastic caps over the idle adjustment screws to prevent amateur tampering with the idle and therefore the possible increased emission of pollutants.

IDLE MIXTURE   The ratio of mixture of fuel and air in the carburetor set at a low or idling engine speed.

IGNITION   The process of burning a mixture of fuel and air in the combustion chamber to create work power.

IGNITION SYSTEM   The collected and individual components which effect ignition in the combustion chamber. These include the battery, ignition switch (key), coil, distributor and spark plugs, as well as all the wires, cables, relays, terminals and associated equipment required for the system to function properly.

IN-LINE ENGINE   An engine design in which the cylinders are arranged in a row or a straight line. Four and six cylinder engines are normally in-line engines whereas an eight cylinder engine is usually arranged in a counteracting "V" formation.

INSTRUMENTS   The gauges on the dashboard which monitor the car's vital functions.

INTAKE MANIFOLD   The pipelines in which the fuel/air mixture is conducted from the carburetor to the combustion chambers.

INTERNAL COMBUSTION ENGINE   The theory and application of containing an explosion in a closed area and harnessing the resultant power to move a piston which turns a shaft to provide pushing or motive power. At the present time all automotive engines use the internal combution principle, even the Wankel engine. Some engines, however, employ different external configurations or means of fuel intake.

JET   A small tube or nozzle within a carburetor through which fuel flows and is metered.

JUMPER CABLES   A means by which a car with a dead battery can still be started by connecting its electrical system to the good battery in another car with a set of two cables.

KEROSENE   Another petroleum derivative formerly used as a fuel and now chiefly used as a cleaning solvent.

KICKDOWN SWITCH   Commonly called "passing gear," this is a switch in the carburetor whereby flooring the gas pedal and opening the carburetor wide causes the automatic transmission to shift down into the next lower gear for increased passing power.

KNOCK   A tapping or rattling sound in the engine caused by incorrect ignition timing or by loose or bad engine parts such as bearings.

LEAF SPRING   A method of suspending the car body from the frame and axles. This type of spring is used only on the rear suspension of most cars.

LEAN MIXTURE   A lean mixture, as opposed to a rich mixture, is when a low ratio of fuel to air is mixed by the carburetor.

LIMITED SLIP DIFFERENTIAL   A type of driveshaft and rear axle gear arrangement whereby the right and left rear wheels can rotate independently rather than at the same speed. This allows at least one wheel to find traction should the other wheel be spinning on ice, for example.

LININGS   These are the brake shoe pads and they are called linings because they can be removed from the shoes when worn. New linings are then riveted to the old shoes and this is called "having the brakes relined" in the auto service business.

LUBE JOB   This job is normally done when the oil is changed and it involves greasing the suspension and steering joints and fittings.

LUBRICANT   Technically speaking any slippery substance is a lubricant including engine oil and heavy grease.

LUBRICATING SYSTEM   The system and components which hold, pump, distribute and recirculate oil throughout the engine: the oil pan, oil pump, oil passages, oil filter, oil pressure indicator gauge and the oil itself.

LUG NUTS The nuts which, by screwing onto studs, hold the wheel onto the hub on the end of the axle.

MAGS Mags are chrome-like wheels favored by hot rodders. They are called "mags" because they are often made of magnesium for weight-saving purposes.

MAIN BEARINGS See "Bearings." The main bearings are the ones which hold and support the crankshaft in the bottom of the engine.

MANIFOLD A pipe which connects one inlet to several outlets or connects several inlets to one outlet. An intake manifold connects one inlet (the carburetor) to several outlets (each cylinder). The exhaust manifold connects several inlets (each cylinder) to one outlet (the exhaust pipe).

MASTER CYLINDER The main brake fluid reservoir of the brake system from which fluid is pressure-pumped to each wheel cylinder to effect a hydraulic reaction—the expansion of the brake shoes.

MISFIRING A situation in which there is no explosion in the combustion chamber due to some failure in the ignition system. The fuel then passes right through the chamber unburned.

MIXTURE The ratio of fuel to air created in the carburetor.

MUFFLER A device fitted somewhere in the exhaust system of a car and constructed to dull the very loud noise created by a running engine.

NEGATIVE The ground side of the battery or of the electrical circuit.

NUTS Usually in combination with bolts, as nuts and bolts. The nut is a donut-shaped object which is threaded on its inside edge and screws down over the threaded outside end of a bolt.

OCTANE A system used to grade fuel according to its antiknock qualities.

OHM A method used to measure the resistance to current flow in an electrical circuit.

OIL Any liquid lubricant but chiefly the oil used to lubricate an engine.

OIL CAPACITY The amount (in quarts) of oil that an engine's lubricating system requires.

OIL FILTER   A replaceable canister in which a gauzy mesh removes impurities from the oil in the lubricating system.

OIL PAN   The large tank on the bottom of the engine which is the collection and pumping reservoir for the engine oil.

OIL PUMP   A small mechanical device which picks oil up from the oil pan and pumps it up into those parts of the engine which need to be lubricated.

OUT-OF-ROUND   A condition where something that is supposed to be perfectly round, such as a piston, a cylinder, a bearing, or a tire, is not.

OVERDRIVE   An extra gear for a transmission. For example, shifting from high gear to overdrive requires less work of the engine to maintain the same speed.

OVERSTEER   A handling situation common in rear-engined cars where the greater weight of the rear end of the car causes the rear to, in effect, try to pass the front of the car.

PARKING LIGHTS   The small, white or amber lights at the front of the car and the taillights. Pulling the headlight switch halfway out normally activates the parking lights.

PCV VALVE   PCV stands for Positive Crankcase Ventilation and it is a method of recirculating waste gases from inside the engine back through the combustion process rather than letting them out into the atmosphere.

PETROLEUM   Crude oil—the substance which is pumped out of the ground and which can then be refined into a wide variety of forms such as oil, gasoline and kerosene.

PING   A rattling, knocking sound in the engine caused by a poor state of tune or by using gasoline of too low an octane.

PISTONS   The barrel-shaped devices inside the cylinder which are forced downward by the combustion explosion and which turn the crankshaft via a connecting rod.

PISTON RINGS   A series of bracelets round the upper outside of each piston which make a better seal between the piston and the cylinder wall. Piston rings serve two main purposes: they keep the force of combustion from leaking down around the piston and thereby dissipating and they also keep the lubricating oil from leaking up into the combustion chamber and burning. Often when you see a car which smokes a lot it is because these rings are worn and oil is being burned with the gasoline.

PLAY   The amount of movement in a mechanical device. This term is often used when referring to automotive steering and front-end operation. Steering wheel play is the amount the wheel can be turned side-to-side before the front wheels begin to turn.

POINTS   The set of contacts inside a distributor which open and close the electrical circuit from the coil.

POSITRACTION   This is a limited slip differential and may be called by various names for different types of cars. This device allows the rear wheel which can get traction to do so when driving on ice or any slippery surface. Otherwise, both rear wheels would spin if one cannot get traction.

POWER STEERING   A mechanical and hydraulic system whereby the process of turning the front wheels is made easier.

POWER TRAIN   Those components of an automobile which are related to propelling it. They include the engine, transmission, driveshaft (clutch), differential and rear axle.

PRE-IGNITION   This action occurs when there is a combustion explosion before the spark plug fires. The cause of this is rather complex but is related to a poorly tuned engine.

PRESSURE   The force of an external object or substance against something. Also the internal force of a substance created by expansion or compression.

PRESSURE CAP (Radiator)   The removable filler/cover for the radiator which can be removed yet when replaced seals the radiator so pressure can build up inside.

PULLEY   A grooved wheel used to transmit power from the source to another place through an attaching belt.

PULLING   A front end or brake system term used to describe a situation in which the car jerks to either side when the brakes are applied.

RADIATOR   A large receptacle mounted in front of the engine and fan through which water circulates to be cooled after coming out of the engine.

RADIATOR CAP   See "Pressure cap."

RADIATOR CORE   The lower part of the radiator which consists of rows of tubing finned for cooling ease.

RADIATOR HOSES   The upper and lower rubber tubes which connect the radiator to the engine. The upper hose conducts water from the engine back to the radiator and the lower hose conducts water from the radiator into the engine.

REAR   When mechanics speak of "the rear" or "the rear end," they are referring to the differential and rear axle assembly.

RECALL   When the manufacturer of an auto discovers a design or construction error, cars already purchased are "recalled" to the nearest dealer to have the problem remedied.

RECAP   A process by which new treads are mounted onto an old tire. With today's big cars and high speeds, this practice is not as common as it was in the past.

REGISTRATION   The act of licensing autos by a state or the card representing this licensing.

REGULATOR   An electrical device in the car's electrical system which monitors and adjusts the voltage put out by the alternator.

RESISTANCE   This is an electrical term which refers to the ability of a conductor (such as a wire) to oppose current coming through it. Copper would have a low resistance and rubber would have high resistance.

REVOLUTIONS PER MINUTE (RPM)   This is a very common method of measuring various engine functions and it refers to the number of times the crankshaft goes around in one minute.

RETARD   Moving back the timing of each spark plug's ignition.

RICH MIXTURE   This refers to the ratio of fuel to air in the carburetor and it denotes a higher than normal ratio of gasoline to air.

RIM   The wheel of a car minus the tire is often called the rim.

ROTARY ENGINE   An internal combustion engine but one with a very different mechanical process lacking pistons, connecting rods and a conventional crankshaft.

ROTOR   The device on the inside top of the distributor which rotates and in doing so sends electrical impulses to the different cables and on to the spark plugs.

Disc brake systems also have a part called the rotor and this is the disc itself. The rotor spins with the wheel and when you apply the brakes, two pads on either side of the rotor pinch it to stop the wheels from turning. If you pinched a spinning phonograph record with your fingers, you would be imitating the disc brake operation.

SAGGING   In automotive jargon sagging refers to the effect on a car of worn-out springs.

SEALED BEAM   This is the type of headlights found on all of today's autos.

SEIZING   If your car's engine runs out of the oil necessary to cool it and lubricate its operation, the engine will seize. This means that the pistons and cylinder walls will become so hot that they expand and the piston can no longer move up and down. If this happens, the engine will be permanently ruined.

SELF-ADJUSTING BRAKES   These are drum brakes which can adjust themselves by being applied when the car is backing up and the wheels are turning backwards.

SENDING UNIT   These are the other ends of the gauges on the dashboard. For example, a measuring device within the engine determines the oil pressure and sends that information to the oil pressure gauge on the dash. Each gauge has a sending unit of some type.

SHEET METAL   This is the body or outside metal surface of the car including the fenders, hood, doors and trunk.

SHIFT   To change gears in the transmission, or the lever inside the car by which the gears are changed.

SHIFT LINKAGE   The mechanism which connects the shift to the transmission.

SHIMMY   Another front-end term which describes a vibration caused by misalignment of the front wheels or worn front suspension or steering parts.

SHOCK ABSORBER   A hydraulic (fluid-filled) device situated near each wheel and spring which absorbs road shocks and spring vibrations.

SHOE   A part of a drum brake system. Each of the four brakes has two shoes which expand outward and rub against the drum to stop the wheel from turning.

SHORT CIRCUIT   A path of least current resistance which allows the current to take a path other than its designated one, i.e., a break in a wire which allows contact with another component.

SHROUD   A fiberglass, plastic or sheet metal hood surrounding the fan. This is strictly a safety device to prevent personal injury.

SLIP   A term narmally used to describe improper clutch action.

SOLENOID   A switching device used to operate the starter motor.

SPARE   The fifth tire stowed in the trunk and used to replace a flat on one of the four driving tires.

SPARK   Ignition or the igniting flame caused by firing the spark plug.

SPARK KNOCK   See "Ping."

SPARK PLUG   There is one spark plug for each cylinder or combustion chamber. They serve as the devices which conduct the high voltage electrical current to the two electrodes and cause a big spark between the electrodes.

SPECIFICATIONS (Specs)   The list of gaps, measurements, sizes and settings which describe the optimum relationships of components and systems for your specific car. These include: the spark plug gap, the spark plug type, distributor dwell angle, point gap, ignition timing setting, valve openings and idle speed settings.

SPEEDOMETER   The dashboard gauge which indicates the number of miles per hour the car is traveling. The actual miles per hour measurement is taken by a sending unit in the transmission or driveshaft.

SPRINGS   The devices used to suspend the car body from the frame and axles. Most American cars use leaf springs in the rear and coil springs in the front.

STALLING   When the engine stops running due to a lack of fuel, air or electric current.

STARTER   A small, high-speed electric motor which rotates the engine fast enough to be able to keep going on its own power.

STARTER SWITCH   The ignition key which activates the starter motor.

STARVING   The condition in the carburetor which consists of too much air and not enough fuel. An overly lean mixture.

STEERING   The series of devices which allow the driver to control the direction of the two front wheels by turning a wheel in the car.

Power Steering   See "Power Steering."

Manual Steering   A strictly mechanical method of steering, unassisted by power devices.

STROKE   A measurement of the total distance travelled by the piston from its highest to lowest point in the cylinder.

SURGING   A charging motion of the engine caused by an improper injection of gasoline by the carburetor.

SUSPENSION   The system used to connect the car body to the frame and axles, including the springs and shock absorbers.

SYNCHROMESH   A system of synchronizers in a manual transmission which allow the driver to downshift (4th to 3rd to 2nd to 1st) without grinding the gears.

TACHOMETER   An instrument used to measure the revolutions per minute produced by the engine.

TAILLIGHTS   The red lights at the extreme rear of the car which light up with the parking lights and with the head lights.

TAIL PIPE   That part of the exhaust system which carries exhaust from the muffler to the rear of the car and out.

TAPPETS   The valve lifter. This is a connecting device: it is pushed up by the camshaft lobe and it in turn pushes up the valve (exhaust and intake) so it can open to let fuel in or exhaust out.

TERMINAL   A connection or junction in an electrical circuit.

THERMOMETER   A device used to measure temperature, usually in Fahrenheit degrees.

THROTTLE   The device in the carburetor (often called the butterfly valve) which controls the mixture flow from the carburetor to the intake manifold.

THROW-OUT BEARING   One of the parts of the clutch on a standard transmission which causes the transmission shaft to be disengaged from the engine.

TIE-ROD   A rod which connects two parts together so that they can pivot, such as the steering gears and the front wheels.

TIMING   The regular frequency of an event such as the firing of the spark plugs or the opening and closing of the valves.

TIMING LIGHT   A tool used when tuning up the engine; it flashes on and off exactly when the number one spark plug fires and thereby allows you to set the valve timing accordingly.

TIRES   The rubber covers for the wheels which are filled with air and therefore absorb road shocks and make the ride soft as well as providing good traction on hard surfaces.

Belted Bias   A method of tire construction whereby an additional layer of tread is placed at an angle to the basic layer.

Bias Ply   The standard old method of tire construction with crisscrossing plies.

Radial Play   Like belted bias tires but with an additional belt running circumferentially around the tire.

Tube & Tubeless   In the past, tires had inner tubes within them to hold the pressurized air. Nowadays the tire itself is sealed to the rim and keeps the air in by itself.

TOLERANCE   The clearance or variation in size that a part can tolerate before its function is affected.

TORQUE   A measure of the available twisting force. The rotating ability of the engine is measured in foot pounds, as opposed to pushing or pulling power measured in horsepower. Your ability to unscrew the top of a jar is your torque.

TRANSMISSION   One component of the power train which, through various gears and shafts, transforms the usable power generated by the engine into particular functions such as the different forward speeds, reverse and neutral.

TROUBLESHOOTING   A careful and methodical system-by-system examination of the automobile to pinpoint an operational problem.

TUNE-UP   A maintenance operation which is performed periodically to restore the engine's performance which deteriorates due to wear on parts and loss of adjustment. A tune-up has three steps: analysis, where the degree of wear and loss of adjustment is determined; parts replacement or repair, where worn or dirty parts are replaced or refurbished; adjustment, where precision engine settings are returned to their original specifications. The three major areas covered in a tune-up are: the ignition system, the fuel system and the engine compression. A valve adjustment may also be included if the particular auto has mechanical valves rather than hydraulic valves.

TURNING RADIUS   The size of the circle created when a car is driven with the steering wheel locked hard to one side or the other. The smaller this circle is, the better—because the car is therefore more responsive to control by the driver.

TURN SIGNALS   A warning blink of the left or right taillights and front parking lights to indicate the driver's intention to make a left- or right-hand turn; these blinks are activated by a lever on the left side of the steering wheel column.

UNDERSTEER   This is the opposite of oversteer and it is the tendency of a front engined car (all American cars) to plow into a corner. If an understeering car goes into a corner too fast, it will slide sideways while an oversteering car will begin to spin around, back first, when entering a corner too fast.

UNIVERSAL JOINTS   Commonly called just "U-Joints," these are found at either end of the driveshaft and connect it to the transmission and to the differential. Their purpose is to make the drive train flexible because the engine and transmission are bolted to the frame while the rear axle is connected to the frame by springs almost constantly in motion.

VACUUM   The suction effect created by pumping air out of an enclosed receptacle. When the carburetor pumps air and fuel out of itself and into the combustion chambers, a vacuum is created.

VALVES   In most cars, each combustion chamber has two valves: one intake valve and one exhaust valve. Their purpose is to open and close at the proper times so that fuel can be taken in for combustion and exhaust can be expelled after combustion.

VALVE COVER(S)   These are simply metal covers which contain the valve system, keep it clean and keep the engine oil inside. They are long (the length of the top part of the engine) and rounded over the top. In-line engines have one running the length of the top and V-8's have two: one for the top of each side.

VALVE JOB   Adjusting the amount by which the valves open and close, grinding and cleaning worn or carbon covered valves, or replacing bent or completely worn valves.

VAPOR   The gaseous state (as opposed to liquid) of any substance.

VAPOR LOCK   A fuel line condition which usually occurs on a very hot day where the fuel heats to the point of expansion and blocks normal flow.

V-8 ENGINE   The type of engine found in many modern American autos, the V-8 design provides eight cylinder power and smoothness but in a smaller area than would be required by an in-line 8 cylinder design. Rather than the pistons going straight up and down, they are in a V-shaped design (four to a side) at 90° to each other.

VELOCITY   A moving object's rate of speed.

VIBRATION   Short, regular movements of a part in any direction, usually undesired.

VISCOSITY   A rating of measure of the thickness or thinness of a liquid, usually only used when referring to oil.

VISE   A tool which is securely bolted to a workbench and which can be opened and tightly closed to hold the item being worked on firmly in place.

VOLTAGE   A measurement of electrical pressure or current force.

VOLTMETER   An instrument used to measure voltage in a circuit.

VOLUME   The amount of space that can be occupied within a chamber or receptacle.

WANDERING   The tendency of a car to drift from its straight ahead or aimed direction, usually the result of front end misalignment or improperly inflated front tires.

WARRANTY   The guarantee given to the purchaser by an auto manufacturer, usually 12 months or 12,000 miles.

WATER JACKETS   These are the passages within the engine through which the coolant circulates. I assume they are called jackets because in effect they jacket or surround the cylinders where the greatest heat is produced.

WATER PUMP   This device is mounted on the upper front of the engine. It is driven by a belt and pulleys from the bottom of the engine. Coolant is fed into it from the radiator and it pumps that coolant throughout the engine and the rest of the cooling system and back to the radiator for recooling.

WHEELBASE   The distance between the front and rear axles of an automobile, usually measured in inches. Naturally, this distance will be quite a bit shorter than the total length of the car.

WHEELS   The steel discs which are mounted onto both the ends of each axle and onto which the tires are mounted.

Wheel Balancing   Making sure the the wheel and tire rotate in a completely flat plane around the axle hub by adding weight to different places on the wheel.

Wheel Bearings   Wear-resistant and grease-filled metal rollers within which the axle turns.

Wheel Cylinders   The receptacles at each wheel which fill with brake fluid from the master cylinder and expand, causing the brake shoes to also expand and rub against the drums to stop the wheel from turning.

WINDSHIELD   The safety glass body insert at the front of the car for outside visibility and inside protection.

Windshield Washer   The system by which water and cleaning solvent is pumped from an underhood receptacle onto the windshield so that wiper action can clean the windshield.

Windshield Wipers   The metal arms and rubber blades which sweep back and forth across the windshield to give visibility in the rain and snow. The wipers are driven by a small electric motor beneath the windshield.

WRENCH   Although there are many types of wrenches, they all serve a similar purpose: to loosen or tighten nuts and bolts. Some of the types of wrenches are: open-end wrenches, box wrenches, combination open-end and box wrenches, socket wrenches, nut drivers, adjustable wrenches, allen wrenches and torque wrenches.

Chapter 1

Your Car

The Car As An Investment To Be Maintained

Outside of a home, a car is one of the largest investments you will ever make. Next to a home, it is the thing you will live in most of the time. It is also one of the most rapidly depreciating products you

will ever buy so if not properly maintained, it will lose value at an even more alarming rate. When well maintained, it can give you many years of economical pleasure and service. When a car's age reaches five years, it can be worth anywhere from zero to hundreds of dollars and this is directly dependent upon its condition.

It is quite possible to buy a clean secondhand car and do any required repairs yourself; and if you continue to maintain it well, you can sell it for what you paid after a couple of years' use.

You should be just as much a consumer shopper when buying a car as when grocery shopping.

When purchasing a new car, certain equipment will make the car worth more when you sell or trade it, even after providing you with the extra conveniences while you own it. It is not a good idea to buy a large car without power steering, power brakes, automatic transmission and air conditioning. On the other hand, most small cars are easy to drive without power steering, and they are light enough to stop without power brakes. But the horsepower is lower and therefore it takes more of what is available to drive an air conditioner, automatic transmission, and other power accessories.

When it comes to accessories such as an adjustable steering wheel, a six-way power seat, electric door locks, etc., I think they are convenient but don't add enough to the trade-in value and, of course, they provide that many more systems and components to break or wear out. By mentioning all this I don't mean that it is best to go out and buy a standard, stripped down economy car. You may save when you buy but resale value will be that much lower.

Therefore, when you do buy a car, think very carefully about the price, the overall condition (if used), options (their real value and their cost), personal suitability, economy and potential depreciation rate.

Remember, no matter who you buy from they are in business to make as much money as they can. This applies to a private sale as well as a dealer. So you must be a tough, consumer-minded shopper when purchasing a car. Most women shop for grocery bargains to save a few dollars a month. One would hope that you would apply the same zeal to car shopping in order to save a few hundred dollars. To most women the whole process of buying a car, especially if financing it, is so technical, complicated and

generally mystifying that they are simply anxious to get the car and go. But you, after reading this book, will know enough to deal with the car seller on his level and this might well be worth a lot of money to you.

Never, never buy a car which is being sold "as is." This usually means trouble and the dealer or owner doesn't want anything more to do with it. Always get a thirty day written guarantee on a used car and always take it to your own garageman and have him check the automobile over before you buy.

Loans

Personally, I think the best way to buy a car, if you don't have ready cash, is to borrow from a bank. Usually, a bank will finance two-thirds the price of the car for one to three years. The amount financed and the period of time depends on the year of the car, the character of the borrower and, of course, the individual bank.

Most banks finance new cars for 36 months at anywhere from 7–14% interest. A bank will require the borrower to have fire, theft and collision insurance on the car in order to protect the car—which you put up as collateral for the loan. Therefore, even if you have an accident with someone who has no insurance, your company will pay back the bank loan.

Bank rates are traditionally lower than those of loan companies who may charge up to 25% interest—yes, 25%.

New car dealerships also offer their own financing plans and their interest rates fall somewhere between the banks and the loan companies. When you buy a new car the salesman will probably try to sell you on financing at the dealership because he gets a commission on that too.

But don't assume that all banks, all dealers, or all loan companies have the same rates—they may all differ and some may overlap so check several of each. Like household shopping, you must be a comparison shopper.

Does It Fit You?

Like people, cars come in different sizes, colors and dispositions. As in choosing most products, one person's likes are another's dislikes: some like small cars while others prefer large ones. I meet many women here in the garage who would never own a large car. They feel that the big cars are hard to park, difficult to maneuver and a strain to see out of. These women are swallowed up by a big car and they feel that the smaller cars are easier to park, able to scoot through traffic and more responsive to the wishes of the driver. Small cars usually get better gas mileage, which is extremely important these days, and they are often cheaper to repair than large autos.

On the other hand, many women who own large cars do so because they feel that they are safer and more comfortable and that they are made better and therefore last longer than the smaller cars. Both sides have sound arguments in their favor so if you are considering a new car, don't make up your mind solely on esthetic appeal: evaluate your purchase relative to your preferences, your size, your pocketbook, your driving habits and your intended use of the car.

Does Your car fit you?

Regardless of what you choose, there are ways to make it feel safer and fit you more comfortably. Women who are short like me may have trouble trying to see fenders over the steering wheel of a large car. This can be corrected to some degree by raising the front seat with blocks or washers, moving the front seat tracks forward and simply by adjusting the seat back and forth. If you have short legs, the brake pedal and accelerator pedal may be extended to meet your needs. In addition, many new cars offer a telescoping steering wheel and/or adjustable pedals as options to provide you with a more comfortable and safer driving position.

This discussion of what fits you and what you like will probably be secondary to what you can beg, borrow or steal but keep it all in mind when buying a car of your own or when buying a "family car" of which you will be the principal driver.

Driving Habits and Intended Uses

It is almost universal in America for a car to be purchased according to its image, status or physical appearance; little emphasis is placed on its utility value. However, with the cost of automobiles constantly increasing and with the cost of operating them increasing even faster (gas, service, insurance, etc.), buyers should evaluate a new car very, very carefully and match it to their habits and intended uses.

If, for example, you use a car only to drive to the train station or to drive a short distance to work, buying a large luxury car would be neither smart nor practical. On the other hand, if you are a traveling saleswoman, buying the tiniest economy car might not be practical for highway driving. If you have a large family to transport, you may have to buy a station wagon but even there you can choose from many types and sizes. In fact, there are 25 models of American station wagons and 18 models of foreign station wagons offered for sale in this country so in just the wagon area there are 43 different models to select among—many quite unique in construction, size, price, options and utility value. These facts and figures only make the point that you should give very serious thought to what you personally will require of a car over the period which you own it and buy accordingly.

Right or Left

From now on, why don't you try to use the correct terminology when referring to your car? Let's start, elementary as it may sound, with which is right and which is left on your auto.

As you sit in the car facing forward, your left hand is left and your right hand is right. This might seem obvious but the point is that these right and left designations remain the same no matter how you are looking at the car. Some folks don't know this for we have had people come in and say: "That right front tire is down," while pointing to the left front tire. This may not seem like a big

deal unless you are the mechanic who has to go by notes from customers. So, to get the best service for your money, give your mechanic the best description and instructions possible. A detailed description of your car's problems will save the mechanic analysis time and trial-and-error repairs and, as you know, repair costs are based on time as well as the cost of parts.

Tools

All new cars come equipped with a jack and a lug wrench. Instructions for operating the jack and changing a spare tire can be found in your owner's manual or pasted inside the trunk. If neither of these are available, refer to Chapter Three where I tell how to change a flat tire. In order to be prepared for the worst, you should try this equipment in your own driveway to see how it works; or have your gas station attendant demonstrate it for you using your own car's jacking equipment. In any case, make sure that the correct tools are in fact in the car and in working condition. This equipment should also stay with the car when you sell it so the new owner won't be stranded on the road. By the same token, if you buy a used car, make sure that the previous owner paid you the courtesy of leaving the tools in the car.

For your own safety and convenience you should also carry:

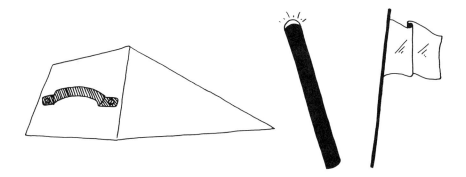

1. *One set of wheel chocks.*   These are triangular pieces of wood which you place in front of or behind the tire opposite the jack when you are fixing a flat. They prevent the car from rolling off the jack and are especially valuable on any sloping road.

   2. *Three red flares or flags.*   These can be used to mark a disabled car on the roadside and/or to signal passing motorists that you need help. Set the flags or flares on the roadside between your car and the oncoming traffic so drivers will see them in time to react to the situation.

   3. *A flashlight.*   A flashlight has a million uses in a car so make sure you have one and that its batteries are strong.

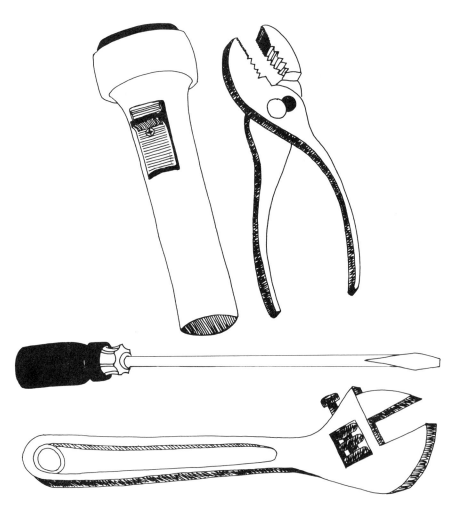

   4. *A good pair of pliers, a screwdriver, a small hammer and an adjustable wrench.*   If you can fix a small and obvious problem yourself, you save the high cost of road service; so be prepared by having these basic tools in the car.

5. *A fire extinguisher.* The obvious use is to put out a fire but it can also be used to rout an assailant.

6. *A white cloth.* This is not a crying towel but a signal to hang on the outside driver's door handle to show that you need help.

For better or worse, girls, chivalry is dead and the days of raising your skirt above your knee to attract male help are just about gone. Today every skirt is above the knee—no wonder guys don't seem to have the time to help a female in distress.

Another item still available but not used much nowadays are tire chains. Since studded tires came out, chains aren't used too often because they are hard to put on. But I'll say one thing: they will go places where a snow tire or a studded tire will not. So if your neck of the woods gets a lot of snow or if studs are illegal in your state, chains are the answer.

Spray de-icers, an ice scraper and a small whisk broom are handy things to have, particularly if your car is outside in the winter.

A set of battery jumper cables should complete your tool kit. These are not absolutely necessary but they can come in very handy if a passing motorist or a neighbor is willing to give you a jump start.

Keys

I'm sure you have seen the television ads that advise you not to help a good kid go bad by leaving your keys in the car. Well, statistics show that many stolen cars are taken because keys were left in them. Make it a habit to always remove the car keys and lock the doors when you leave the car.

The keys to your car are as important as your house keys, if not more so. You can break a window to get into your home but if you break a car window to get in, you still can't drive it without the key. You will just sit there even unable to play the radio. Many times we foolishly lose keys while shopping but this is where a little foresight can save you a lot of trouble.

Hide two extra keys (ignition and trunk keys) under the front or rear bumper, in back of the license plate or in any other good place you think of *outside* the car. Just be sure to remember where you hide them. You can get small, magnetic key boxes at most auto stores and they are cheap and made for this purpose. One great place to hide it is under the hood—providing that your hood release is not inside the car.

Garage

Do you have one? Well, if you don't, I wouldn't worry too much although it does protect paint and keep the car dry. Any car is easier to start when protected against the elements, but a well-maintained car will start indoors or out.

Never let your car idle in a garage with the doors closed since carbon monoxide, which is a killer, will fill up the garage. Above all when you are going in or out of your garage, make sure the car doors are closed tight. This may sound belittling but an awful lot of car doors are badly damaged by hitting the side of the garage while the driver is holding the door open to look where he is backing. Be especially watchful for toys or bicycles in the driveway— particularly a bicycle with a child riding it.

Lots of men come to our garage and say: "Oh, the old lady hit the side of the garage," or, "She backed out with the door open." It's always *she* never *he.* That nasty term "woman driver" bit the dust long ago so keep your eyes open, be careful, and make sure you do not become the brunt of some bad joke.

Always make sure your car is all the way in or all the way out of the garage because if you have an overhead door, anyone can put it down and dent your trunk. If you have side closing doors, the wind can catch them and dent the car or break the doors. This has happened and it can be, very expensive for body work and carpentry—a fact which can be verified by your insurance company.

Information, Please

Questions are always raised as to how much air should be put in the tires, how much oil in the engine and the location and operation of gadgets on the dashboard such as washers, wipers, cruise control, heater, defroster, etc. All of these questions, and many more, will be answered in this book. However, a few basic answers may be found in the handbook that comes with a new car. If you have misplaced this handbook, write to the manufacturer telling him the year and model, and request a new owner's manual or ask your local dealer to obtain one for you.

By the way, if you sell or trade your car, be sure to leave the manual with it for this is a courtesy the buyer will appreciate. Used car dealers love to have the original manual in the car as it can show that the previous owner went by the book and took care of the car.

As an alternative to finding a replacement manual, you can make up your own by finding the appropriate information from your garage or dealer and writing it in the blank spaces provided in the back of this book.

Registration and Inspection

The owner's card or registration card should always be on the person of the driver—not left in the glove compartment. You never know when a police officer is going to stop you and ask for it

along with your driver's license. If your car is ever stolen, the thief will certainly appreciate having the owner's card left for him.

Aside from showing who is the owner of the vehicle, a registration card contains the vehicle identification number and the engine serial number as well as the date of registration. So this is where to go should you ever need this information.

Some states have a regular vehicle inspection, usually in six month periods, such as in my state, Pennsylvania. A sticker is affixed to the windshield when the car passes inspection. In some states inspections are done by licensed local garages and gas stations; in other states inspections are performed by the state itself, usually the state police. But no matter who does it, an owner's card has to be produced and the car must meet the state specifications before it can be operated legally. Don't leave it up to anyone else to follow through on this. The back of the sticker tells when it has expired or is due to expire so get it done at your convenience instead of waiting for the last minute and having the inspection done at the garage's convenience.

Every year I get the postponers on the last day and they line up for blocks to get their sticker. Naturally, this is aggravating to the inspector but it can also be a great inconvenience to you because if you find on the last day of the inspection period that you need work done to pass, you might have to wait for a few days while the garage finishes their other inspections. During those few days you won't be legally able to operate the car, so do yourself a favor—call ahead, make an appointment and get the job over with. Far from being a method of annoying citizens, this inspection is required to insure that automobiles on the road will be as safe as possible—for the driver as well as for everyone else on the road.

Insurance

In most states, some form of minimum insurance is required of all vehicle owners so you ought to familiarize yourself with what you have or what you should have. Where automobiles are concerned, there are generally two areas of insurance: liability and collision.

Liability
This is insurance which you buy to protect your estate (ALL your assets) from any lawsuit by someone you injure. For you to be liable, you must be proven negligent. In most states if both parties are partly to blame, no one person is liable.

Comprehensive Collision
This is insurance which you buy to cover any damage that may happen to your car. It includes anything from a horse eating your convertible top to fire, theft, vandalism and, of course, a collision with another car or with anything else. You can buy collision insurance with whatever deductible amount you wish. When you hear about "$100 deductible," it means that your insurance company, as part of your contract, will pay for damages to your car above and beyond $100. So if your car is worth $2,000 and an accident causes $400 damage, the company will pay you $300 toward having it fixed. If, however, your car is worth $1,000 and accident damages amount to $1,200, your company will pay you $900 or the "total" value of the car. "Total" is a term used in the insurance industry to say that the damages meet or exceed the "book" (wholesale) value of the car. Usually if the damages exceed 70% of the value of the car, the insurance company will "total" the

car and pay you the full value of the car less deductible. Deductible amounts may be $50, $100, $200, etc. (you, the purchaser, decide on the amount). Generally, the higher the deductible, the lower the premiums.

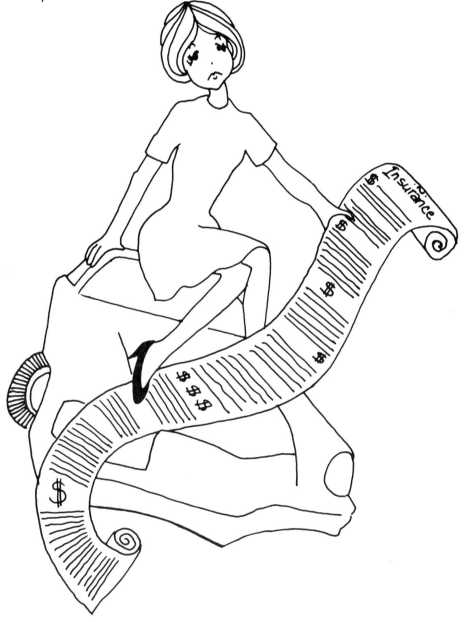

If you have an accident and are not at fault, get your company to pay for the damages to your car and you pay the deductible. Then your company will sue the other person's insurance company for the total amount of damages (repair costs plus deductible) and reimburse you for the deductible amount. If the accident is your fault, your insurance company will pay for repairs to your car (less deductible) plus repairs and deductible for the other person's car.

The best advice I can give is to buy insurance from a good, dependable, known company with an office or agent nearby who will give you trustworthy service and preferably by someone you know.

No Fault

Many states have required insurance companies operating within that state to subscribe to "no fault" insurance. What this means is that the chances of any licensed driver being involved in an accident at some time are pretty good and in many cases the determination of exactly who is at fault is very difficult. Given this viewpoint, you buy insurance against loss or damage regardless of whose fault it is—up to a certain amount so you still have the opportunity to sue for large personal injuries and hospitalization. If you are involved in an accident and damages to your car are $400 and damages to the other car are $500, your company will pay you $300 and the other person's company will pay him $400 (assuming each has $100 deductible).

Deductible

To explain further why insurance companies have deductible amounts after which they pay the rest, imagine how high insurance premiums would be if you could collect for any damage even as small as a parking lot scratch on the door. Processing costs would be more than repair costs. With the deductible system, you worry about small repairs which you can probably pay for anyway and the insurance policy covers the large repairs and injuries which would really destroy your budget.

Depreciating and Pro-Rating

Depreciation or decline in value is pretty rapid on a new car but the rate of depreciation slows as the car gets older. When a car is wrecked, the amount recovered is based on the book value, which I have referred to earlier, and these values are found in either the Red Book or the Blue Book—those mysterious price books available only to dealers, banks and insurance companies. In these books average retail and average wholesale prices are given for any make, model and year automobile plus variations for the condition of the specific car and any optional equipment it may have such as air conditioning, vinyl top or real leather upholstery.

Know Your Car's Manual

The owner's manual is your car's bible but a lot of people just throw it in the glove compartment with everything else and never read it. This is a big mistake because it will familiarize you with the car, tell you the correct year and model and give you complete operating instructions.

Read and use the owner's manual.

I know of people who have driven their car for several months and still don't know how to operate the heater and defroster. Had they read the manual, where the instrument panel and controls are explained, they would have easily learned how to operate all accessories and gadgets.

Also discussed in the owner's manual are keys and locks, seat and seat belt adjustment and how to clean, lubricate and maintain your particular car. Some even have a minor troubleshooting guide so there is value to be gotten from an owner's manual. Read it and use it.

Chapter 2

Play It Safe

The first thing to do after entering your car is adjust your seat to the proper height and distance. Never do this when the car is in motion or you may at best come to a screeching halt. Then adjust both the inside and outside mirrors so you have a clear view of the

Get in the habit of using both rearview mirrors.

road behind you—not so that you can look at your own hair or see that your wig is on straight. Actually you should do that before you get in the car but we all primp occasionally—just don't do it while moving. Now buckle up the seat belt including the shoulder harness. I know this may ruffle your clothes but most auto accident fatalities would not have occurred if the victim had been wearing a seat belt and shoulder harness. If the thought of being killed in a gory car accident is so repulsive that you don't want to be reminded of it by talk of seat belts, just think of the people who love you and depend on you: your husband, children, parents, boyfriend, relatives or friends and ask yourself again whether wearing a seat belt is worthwhile.

When you are driving a car, especially alone, *all* the doors should be locked and the back windows should be closed. There is nothing so frightening as having a stranger jump into your car— especially if he has a gun.

Lock all the doors.

But safety in driving doesn't just mean making yourself safe from intrusion. It also means driving in such a way that safety is your first consideration, not how fast you get there or how long you can put off getting new tires. Self-preservation and the preservation of the other people on the road should be the first thing you think of. Everything else should be subordinate. Quality driving should be positive and defensive.

Keeping your car in good condition is the first safety rule and the one over which you have the most control. If the steering and tires are in good shape and if you have good visibility from the car, then any other safety measures are those *you* take while operating it. This is the purpose of state inspections and this is one of the purposes of this book: for you to know enough about your car to monitor it and keep it in a safe and reliable condition.

Once you have that part of safety under control, the rest is up to you as a driver. Above I mentioned the concept of "defensive driving." The idea is for all drivers to operate their cars in such a way that they compensate for the mistakes and poor driving of the other drivers on the road. While this attitude doesn't give enough stress to the positive safety measures that each driver should take, it does make the point about keeping the other drivers in mind. If, for example, you see a car waiting at a side street, it would be smart to consider the possibility that the driver may not see you and cut in front of you. If you are aware that this might happen, then you can quickly form a response in your mind to use in case it does happen. There are a million possible situations but they all point to being conscious of what's going on around you so that you will have time to react.

The positive safe driving techniques you can employ are:

1. Keep your eyes on the road and cars ahead of you.

2. Glance in both mirrors regularly to see what's happening behind you.

3. Keep the windows and mirrors clean.

4. Know the condition of the tires.

5. Keep a safe distance from the car ahead.

6. Don't run yellow lights

7. Stop completely at stop signs.

8. Have a good view of the road ahead when passing.

9. Don't ride the brake pedal so that when you do apply the brakes, the brake light will be a real signal that you are slowing or stopping.

Keep all the windows clean.

10. Don't drive if you are very tired, upset, taking medicine or if you have been drinking.

Are you hot under the collar? Did you and your boyfriend have a fight and part in bad moods? Did you have one too many to drink or have you been taking drugs—prescription or otherwise?

Well, look out because a car is coming and you are on the wrong side of the road. First that horrible crash and then silence.

You feel yourself being lifted into an ambulance. How many dead? It's all your fault. One for the road and three for the cemetery.

Well, if you start out in any of these moods or conditions, you would be better off just walking because your emotions, not your natural reflexes, are controlling you and something terrible is bound to happen. It's natural when you're angry to jam the gas pedal to the floor but, of course, when you think about it rationally this doesn't help or solve anything. If you are hashing over the day's events in your mind, especially if they have been upsetting, you have a tendency to ignore lights, stop signs, intersections and other cars.

Drinking or taking medicine dulls your reflexes when you need them most—while operating an automobile. Ask your doctor about driving while taking medicine and I'm sure he'll tell you the risk involved. As for drinking while driving—no one needs to be told about this; we've all seen the television ads, and most of us probably know someone who has been killed or injured or has wrecked a car where drinking has been the cause. Because almost everyone in this country at least takes a social drink now and then, we won't face up to the truth about drinking and driving: it is a killer and directly or indirectly is involved in a huge percentage of automobile accidents.

If you must drink or take medicine, don't drive until it wears off. You and the completely innocent person you could kill will be very thankful.

Starting Off

Always start your car in Park and with the brake *on.* After starting, let it warm up for two or three minutes. The colder the weather, the longer the warm-up should be. If you don't let the car warm up sufficiently, it will cough, sputter and stall leaving you without power steering and power brakes.

Before you move an inch, push your brake pedal to make sure it works. It's embarrassing to move and not be able to stop; it can

be messy also. One of my friends lives on a hill and once when she backed out of her garage and down the driveway, she went to apply the brakes and—surprise—there weren't any. She went right across the street, through a fence and into a field. She could have been hit when she crossed the road backwards but she was lucky. Now, after thinking about that little story, release the emergency brake and put the car in gear.

Now you are all set to enter the vast land of roads, billboards and all kinds of people and drivers—and some are a little wild. Take your time and enjoy the drive but keep in mind that you as a safe driver must compensate for the bad or careless drivers.

Personal Safety and Protection

One of the most important factors in auto transportation today, despite the "idiot" devices (lights, buzzers and other reminders) is you the driver. Most auto safety devices function with little or no attention from you, but some things require your cooperation. Keep the following in mind:

1. Make sure all doors are locked *before* you drive away and *before* you walk away after parking.

2. Fasten your seat belts and make your kids and other passengers do likewise.

3. When you leave your car unattended, put the transmission in Reverse or First gear (standard) or put it in Park (automatic). Remove the key and lock up.

4. Always use the hazard switch when you stop for any reason on the highway or in any unusual place.

5. Always park in well lighted areas.

6. Don't leave packages on the seats.

7. Carry a whistle on your key chain or wherever convenient to scare away an attacker and as a signal for help.

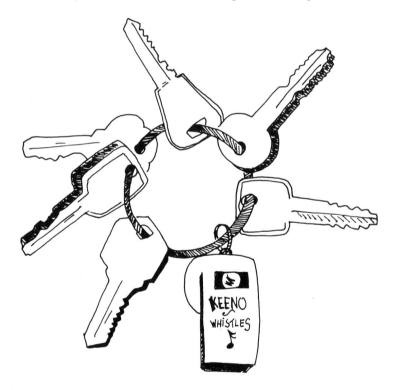

8. Think in terms of your own safety (without becoming paranoid) and avoid potentially unsafe places and situations such as dark parking lots late at night.

9. If stranded in a lonesome spot, wait for help *inside* the car.

With times being the way they are and with seemingly more and more weirdos on the loose, it's better to be safe than sorry. This may not sound like a positive solution to the safe streets problem but keeping yourself alive is a positive beginning. Most newer cars are equipped with four-way flashers, and you should use them anytime you break down. They can serve as a warning to oncoming cars and as an indication that you may need help. I hope you women remember to keep all doors locked at all times and to *never* pick up *anyone* on the road.

Never *pick up hitchhikers.*

Don't leave kids or pets unattended in a car.

If you do break down, get out that white cloth we talked about and hang it on the outside mirror or door handle. This is a sign for help, not surrender. Sit in the car with the doors locked until someone comes. Then just put the window down far enough to talk. Let's not try the leg show and thumb bit or you may be surprised at what stops.

Children and pets should never, ever, be left unattended in cars, especially in hot weather. I have heard of children being burned in car fires caused by playing with lighters; and every summer I read about kids or pets suffocating and dying or suffering brain damage from being left in hot closed cars while mother is in the supermarket for "just a minute."

Chapter 3

On the Road

Starting and Warm-Up

How you go about starting your car, especially on a cold morning, will determine how well it starts and how long it lasts. Keep in mind that the engine is cold (even in the summer) and that engines perform best when they are hot. Therefore, asking too much of a cold engine is also asking for trouble. Also keep in mind that while the engine was not running, all the oil drained back down into the oil pan so revving up a cold engine causes the engine to operate with little or no lubrication. When an engine runs with insufficient lubrication, it is like adding an extra 10,000 miles of wear to the internal parts.

With these scary thoughts in your mind, try to be gentle when starting a cold engine. It doesn't even hurt to be gentle anytime you start the car because many parts are very vulnerable then.

1. Make sure the car is in Park or Neutral.

2. Make sure all accessories are off (radio, heater, wipers, etc.)

3. Pump the gas pedal between two and five times, depending on how cold it is.

4. Hold the gas pedal down about one-third of the way.

5. Turn the starter over with the ignition key.

6. Don't keep cranking if it doesn't catch right away. A series of tries is easier on the battery and the starter motor than prolonged cranking.

7. Let it idle awhile until it idles smoothly. If it won't idle without stalling, pump the gas pedal slightly to keep it going until it will idle by itself.

8. Drive away. The engine will warm up faster while driving rather than sitting at idle but don't race the engine until it is fully warmed. The temperature gauge, temperature light or just plain feel will tell you when the engine is ready for normal performance. It will pay off in long engine life if you go by these indicators.

Roads

Despite high federal, state and local taxes which are supposed to go to road maintenance, many roads in this country leave a lot to be desired. We all know the bone crushing jolt from hitting a large pothole in the road. But such holes and bumps jar more than your teeth; they also jolt the tires, suspension and steering system. One large pothole can damage tires, knock the front wheels out of alignment, strain the springs and break a shock absorber. Even though these parts are designed to resist normal road bumps, a real shock can ruin them. Try to avoid these road hazards and if you do hit an especially bad one, have the front end checked. If the front end alignment is upset, the front tires can wear in half the expected time and that is costly.

It will also pay you to be aware of different road surfaces. The combination of road surface smoothness or roughness and the amount of tread on your tires could cause or prevent an accident. A smooth road will have less friction between it and the tire and make the required stopping distance longer than a rough road surface. When new or almost bald tires are figured into this combination, braking distance and possibility of skidding become much more apparent. When a third factor—rain, snow or ice on the road—is figured in, you can easily see the importance of road awareness. In other words, keep your eyes open, use your head and pay attention to the main task: driving.

If a pothole or a sharp object causes one of the tires to blow out, how you respond can mean the difference between a safe stop and a skidding, careening wreck. If you hear or feel a blowout, the most important thing you can do is *not* apply the brakes. The spinning of the tire will keep some air in it but as it slows, it loses more and more air. If you immediately hit the brakes, you accelerate that process dangerously. If you get a blowout, grip the wheel tightly and concentrate on maintaining steering control. Let your foot off the gas pedal and try to coast to a stop by the side of the road. If you don't have room to coast to a stop, apply the brake very lightly and evenly and steer the wheel as little as possible. Do not, under any but the most extreme conditions, jam on the brakes or the steering wheel will be wrenched right out of your hands and the skidding will start and you will have no control over the car.

Flat Tires

Oh, gosh, a flat tire. Now what? Well, it would be nice if you could always get someone else to stop and change it. When I had my first flat tire, I pulled into a gas station and asked the man if he could please help me. He said: "Nope. I don't change flats." I asked if he could just lift the spare on for me but he said "Nope" again. So I thanked him and changed it myself right in his driveway. It's really not too difficult but, like most endeavors, knowing what to do makes it much easier.

When you get a flat tire, do your best to stop the car on a level surface. Then put on the four-way flashers and hang out the white cloth. If no one stops within a short while, get busy and change it yourself. Having put a pair of work gloves in the trunk would seem pretty smart now, right?

If your car has an automatic transmission, put it in Park; if it has a standard transmission, put it in Reverse. Pull the emergency brake on and shut the engine off.

Now get those little wooden blocks out of the trunk. If you don't have them, bricks or rocks will substitute. Put them in front of (or behind) the tire that is diagonally opposite the flat tire. This keeps the car from rolling forward or backward while up on the jack.

At this point, read the tire changing directions which are glued inside the trunk lid or in your owner's manual. These directions will show you where to place the jack under the bumper (where most of them fit), under the side where some are more effective or underneath for the "scissors" type of jack.

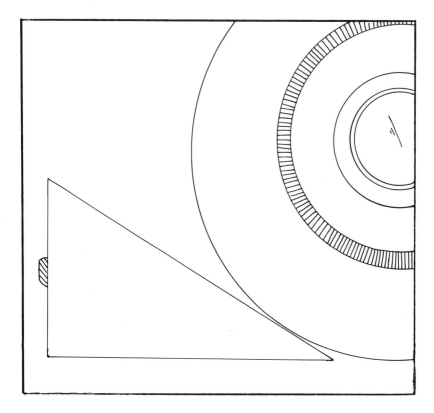

A tire chock.

Remove the spare tire from the trunk by undoing the wing nut that holds the tire in place and then hoisting it out onto the ground. Heavy isn't it? I hope you remembered to check the air pressure periodically.

In most cases, the jack and lug wrench will be in pieces and beneath or behind the spare tire. Take all the pieces out of the trunk and prepare to assemble it. The square part is the base and the jack support tube is the long, serrated piece with the gadget that slides up and down on it. Insert the jack support tube into the base so that the whole apparatus stands upright. Be sure that you put the proper end of the tube into the base; you can tell the proper end because it will be the one opposite the jack arm.

The gadget which slides up and down on the jack support tube is the jack. Protruding from the jack is a short, hollow arm which can be pumped up and down to make the jack climb up and down the support tube. To give the user better leverage, the lug wrench (a long, heavy pipe with a socket on one end) can be inserted into the jack arm. But, when you do this and pump the handle, you will notice that the jack only goes in one direction. To make it go in the opposite direction, look for a little switch on the other side of the jack from the arm, or possibly underneath the arm, and flip it up or down depending on which way you want the jack to go.

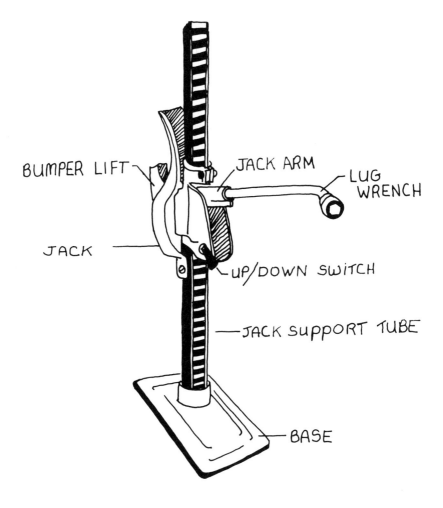

The jack and its parts.

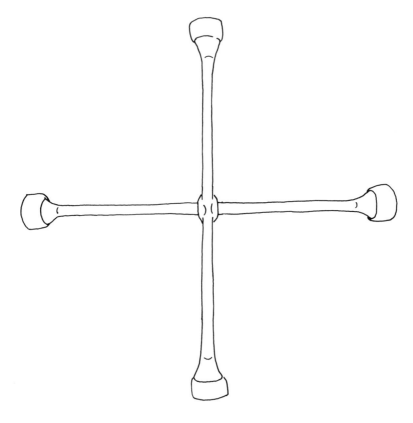

A lug wrench.

Where To Put The Jack

When you have the jack assembled and know how it works, look for that point on the car where the jack fits. Some jacks have a hook shaped front which allows them to fit under the bumper and lift it; these will either fit anywhere on the bumper or there will be holes in the bumper especially for the jack. If your car has a side jack instead of a bumper jack, look for holes just under the sides of the car between the front and rear wheels.

If your car has a scissors jack (so called because it looks like a scissors as it opens), it will fit under the frame or under the axles. You raise this type of jack by attaching the lug wrench to one end and turning it to raise the jack and car.

Whichever type you have, place the jacking apparatus under the appropriate jacking point and raise it until it just holds weight but does not lift the tire off the ground.

Now remove the hubcap or wheel cover from the flat tire's wheel using either the opposite, flat end of the lug wrench or a screwdriver. You will see four to six lug nuts which hold the wheel to the hub. These must be removed and that can be accomplished with the socket end of the lug wrench. Before you jack up the car, loosen these lug nuts slightly. If they are really tight, hammer on the wrench with a rock or even stand on it.

Now jack the car up a little bit and remove the lug nuts completely. Sometimes you will come across lug nuts that turn in

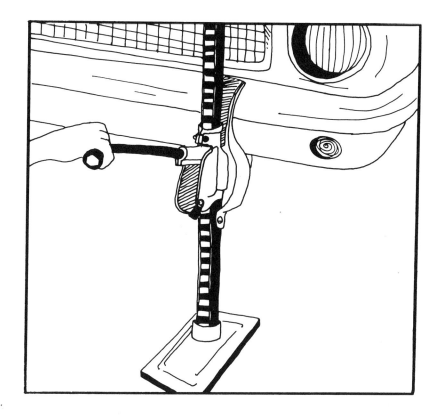

Placing the bumper jack.

the opposite direction from what you think they should. If so, the end of their bolts should be stamped with an "L" or an "R" for Left or Right. Usually the nuts turn left or counterclockwise as you face the flat tire.

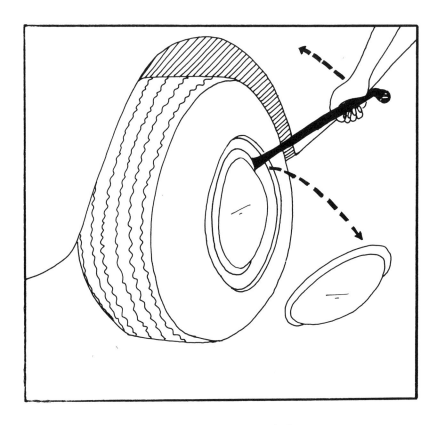

Pry off the wheel cover or hub cap.

As you unscrew the lug nuts put them into the hubcap so you won't misplace them. Jack the car all the way up and pull the flat tire off of the hub and roll it to one side. Then roll the spare over so that it is face down right in front of the empty hub. Stand it up and try to fit it onto the hub. Chances are good that you will have to jack the car up a little more to allow the full tire to fit. Try again and put the spare on just the way the flat came off. For leverage put your screwdriver or lug wrench under the tire and lift up, being careful to align the holes in the wheel with the bolts that stick out of the hub.

Once the tire is on, screw the lug nuts on as far as you can by hand. Tighten them a little more with the lug wrench until doing so begins to make the wheel turn.

Now flip the jack switch to make the jack go down and pump the jack handle, slowly lowering the car to the ground. When the new tire just touches the ground, tighten the lug nuts some more.

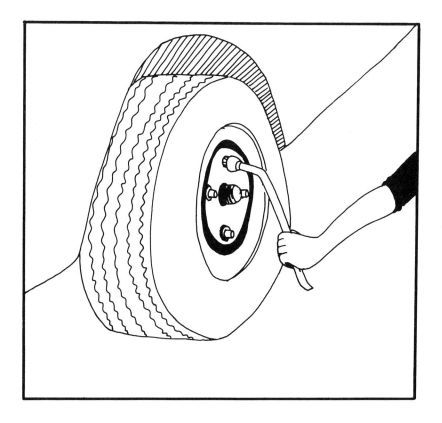

Loosen the lug nuts.

Lower the car completely, remove the jacking apparatus, and again tighten the lug nuts as far as you can. Put the jacking equipment away, put the hubcap in the car and then go to a garage to have it all rechecked. *Voilà!* You changed a tire yourself.

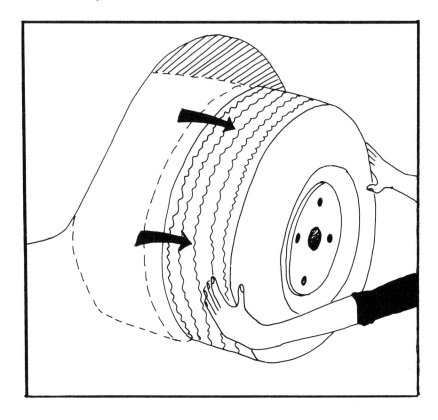

Remove the flat tire.

Weather

Running Through Water

The other day a lady customer came in with an old Mercedes-Benz. She had driven through water and her brakes slipped and slid. I figured that water had gotten into the brakes and, although she had full pedal, the car wouldn't stop. This has been the cause of many accidents because the driver doesn't know that the brakes don't work until she needs them.

If possible, go around a puddle; if not, go through it very slowly and in a low gear. Then, as you come back onto the road, move slowly and hold your foot gently on the brake. This will warm up the brake linings and cause them to dry out. While doing this, keep your distance from other cars.

Another problem arises when running through water: the water may splash up onto the engine and wet the ignition wires, the distributor cap and the spark plugs. Try hard to keep the engine running; it will be rough and probably misfire but it will eventually dry out. If the car stalls despite your efforts, remove the distributor cap (explained in Chapter Five, under The Ignition System) and dry it out with a rag or a tissue. Also dry the ends of the cables where they go over the spark plugs but don't mix up the cables. Be sure to do all this with the key OFF or you'll light up like a Christmas tree.

Winterizing and Summerizing

It is never the wrong season to think of winterizing or summerizing your car. Many cars now have air conditioning and are loaded with all sorts of emission control equipment which build up a great deal of heat. In response to this heat build-up, the engine's cooling system must work much harder.

As you probably know, overheating in the summer can be quite troublesome so things to check are: fan belts, hoses, thermostat, hose clamps, radiator cap and the water pump. If these are all in good shape, drain the radiator through the plug in the bottom, flush it with a garden hose, and refill it with a permanent coolant (antifreeze). You may leave this coolant in the system for two years but be sure to have your service station check the level of freezing protection every fall. Also each spring and fall I recommend adding an antirust solution to the cooling system; this prevents corrosion and lubricates the water pump and is very inexpensive. If your car has air conditioning, remember to keep antifreeze in the system all year round.

The oil in your car's engine can also be affected by weather so in the spring use a heavier oil such as SAE 30 which will become thinner with heat. In the winter use SAE 20 which, slightly thinner,

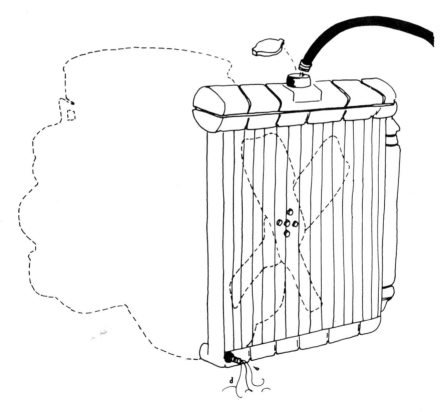

Flushing the radiator.

will make the engine easier to turn over in cold weather. If you live in an extremely cold climate, use SAE 10 as an additive to make the oil lighter and the engine easier to turn over.

The battery water level should be checked every two weeks in the summer and winter. In addition, battery condition should be checked in the spring and fall. Keep in mind that a battery generally lasts for two to three years and hot weather is as hard on a battery as cold weather. High temperatures under the hood evaporate the electrolyte (which is acid) in the battery. Loss of electrolyte exposes the inner plates to air which, in turn, causes them to buckle and sulfate. If water isn't added in time, the battery will be ruined.

Closely related to battery life is the voltage regulator. Regulators on new cars are set for the owner who drives about 12,000 miles a year. Anyone who drives more than this should have the regulator checked and adjusted, if need be, to keep from over-charging the battery or, in some cases, not charging it enough.

Driving In The Snow

If you anticipate driving in the snow, it is always a good idea to load up the trunk of your car as most of the weight in an average car is in the front. You can use cinder blocks or sandbags to make the rear heavier for better traction. You may have noticed that rear-engine cars such as Volkswagens go through the snow much better than cars with the engine in the front. If you are stuck in the snow and you have weight over the rear axle, it is better to back up than to go forward for the simple reason that you would be pulling the front end with the rear wheels instead of pushing the front end deeper into the snow.

Skidding

If your car starts to skid on a rainy, icy or snowy road, remember one cardinal rule: turn the front wheels in the direction of the skid. This does not mean to cut the wheels all the way to either side; how much you point the wheels in the proper direction (toward the direction of the skid) depends on how fast you are going and how severe the skid is. The reason for doing this is to straighten the car out but it is equally important once the car has stopped skidding that you bring the front wheels back to the proper position. Of course, all this takes place in just a few seconds so knowing what to do in advance can prevent a crash and maybe save your life.

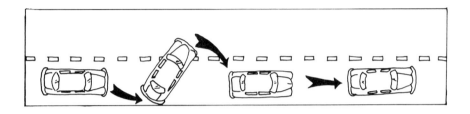

How to stop skidding.

Another winter problem is starting the car on a really cold morning. Your best bet is to turn on the key, pump the gas pedal four or five times and then turn the starter while holding the gas pedal down about one-third of the way. If the car starts but won't move, check the emergency brake. Possibly you left it on the night before and it froze. If this has happened, you can lean under the rear of the car and rap sharply on the back of the wheels with a hammer to break the ice that has formed around the cables. A good practice in winter is to park the car in gear and don't use the emergency brake if possible.

Additives

Whether you should use an additive is a touchy subject because so many people seem, strangely enough, to have strong opinions on this. I honestly believe in some additives such as water pump lubricant, and I like one special oil additive. Good additives are available to free sticky valves and fill hydraulic valve lifters. Also there are commercial solutions which will clean carburetors but if your engine and other equipment is in good condition, additives will not usually make any noticeable improvement. If they do make an improvement, chances are good that the engine has worn to a point that mechanical attention is necessary.

In Case Of An Accident

D-Day has arrived and you've had an accident. What do you do now? First, check to see whether you're O.K. If you are not injured, other than being disarrayed and having your dignity hurt, you will probably be immediately classified as a "woman driver." But remember, the way to dispel that classification is to do your part as a driver and car owner, so get right down to your post-accident responsibilities.

Do not leave the scene of the accident. Have someone call the police immediately and a tow truck if needed. If you have flares and need them, put them out well to the rear of the car so on-coming traffic can see you.

While waiting, get yourself a safe distance off of the road. Do not stay in a car which is on the road as someone may strike it again. If your car is driveable, don't move it until the police arrive. This allows them to measure and, hopefully, verify who is at fault. Make sure you have your operator's license, registration card and insurance information. The police and the other party in the accident will want to see them and they are entitled to do so.

After the accident you will have a specified amount of time to send an accident report to your insurance company and a report to the state. In Pennsylvania an accident report must be filed with the state within twenty-four hours if the damage exceeds $100.00; both parties must file this report.

Accidents and Insurance

If this is your first accident, here are a few facts to help you. First, call the police no matter how minor the damage. This will protect you should the other party suddenly develop a bad back and blame it on the accident.

Second, never say "Oh, it was my fault." No insurance company will permit the policyholder to determine fault. Let the company decide this—which is what you pay them for. I know of an accident where a driver hit another car and dented it slightly. Both parties said nothing was wrong and dropped it. But the outcome was the first driver's insurance company paid a $19,000 lawsuit for whiplash.

Third, be sure to get the names and addresses of the other driver and all witnesses. Give the report to your state and to your insurance company and do nothing else. Particularly do not discuss it with the other party after you have filed reports.

From this stage on, your insurance agent will handle the case. However, be sure to ask him to inform you of all developments and any possible settlements. As the client you have the final word on whether a case goes to court or is settled outside. Often insurance companies will settle out of court if the amount is relatively small in order to keep their legal expenses down and hasten the resolution of the case. But while an out-of-court settlement does not determine fault, it still permits your insurance company to point to your involvement in an accident as a reason for raising your rates. If, on the other hand, the case is settled in court, you are found not at fault and your company pays nothing, then they have no valid reason to raise your rates. Although this is all hypothetical, it makes the point that you should keep yourself informed on what your insurance company is doing and why. And remember—they are your agent and you pay them for insurance and representation services. So keep the nature of the relationship in mind and don't let them bully you.

After the police have done their paperwork at the scene of the accident, you may have the car towed to your own garage. If you are anywhere near home, don't let the driver of the tow truck talk you into having the car towed someplace else. If you are away from your own territory, try to have the car towed to an appropriate dealer.

From this point a claims investigator from your insurance company and from the other party's company will make an estimate of damages or they will ask you to get an estimate, or possibly two, from the shops of your choice.

The police will file a report with the state but be sure to think about any answers or statements you make because if the case goes to court, you will be questioned and expected to give the same answers. Also be sure that you get a copy of the police accident report and that it agrees with your version of the events.

How to Avoid Accidents

The most important advice I can give is always drive ahead of yourself. By this I mean try to forsee oncoming trouble and look for a way out. If, for example, you see someone in a car half way down the block, assume that they are about to open the door and get out. Toot the horn to warn them and be prepared to pass widely to the left or to stop if another car is approaching from the opposite direction. If there are alleys on either side of the street, watch for cars coming out of them. If cars are parked on the street, a child could dart from between them so keep your eyes open and be prepared to stop.

At an intersection you may have the right of way but don't count on it—slow down and look around anyway. Needless to say, running lights that are about to turn red is a bad habit. Tailgating is also a no-no and don't depend on people's turn signals: sometimes they have the left one on but they turn right. Always scan and look ahead and always obey the speed limit. Naturally, ambulances, police cars, fire engines and rescue vehicles always deserve the right of way.

In Case of Breakdown

What To Do Before You Call The Tow Truck

If you have a breakdown on the road and are lucky enough to have someone stop and offer to send help from the next service station, it will be helpful if you know what is wrong so the driver of the tow truck will come prepared. There is a good chance, however, that while trying to figure out what is wrong with your car you may see that you can fix it yourself, at least temporarily. Having a few tools in the car will increase the possibility that you can repair it yourself. First, determine the location of the problem. Is it in the tires, wheels, brakes, steering or suspension? If it is anything there besides a flat tire or a loose wheel, you probably will not be able to fix it well enough to drive the car.

However, if you determine that the power steering drive belt broke, for instance, and can tell that plus the make and model car to the service station, they can probably bring the new belt with them and replace it on the spot. If the car has overheated, you don't have to call for help. Simply turn the car off and let it cool down for fifteen or twenty minutes then head for a garage until it starts to heat up again. If it does, stop again until it cools and continue on.

The procedure to follow when your car breaks down on the road is:

1. Be sure of exactly what happened immediately preceding and during the breakdown.

2. Determine the location and cause of the problem.

3. Decide whether it is something you can fix, at least temporarily, right on the spot.

4. Having made that determination, either fix it and head for a service station for a more permanent repair or begin looking for

help. Remember, road service is expensive so it should be avoided if possible. If you need such service, use your flares or white cloth to signal for assistance. When someone stops, ask them (from inside the car) to please send help from the next service area. Do not, under any circumstances, take a ride with a passing stranger to look for help. It is much smarter to stay with the car in case a repair truck or policeman happens along.

How To Avoid Breakdowns

Avoiding breakdowns is what this book is all about. Keep your car like yourself: in good condition.

Here are a few tips:

1. Keep all fluids at the proper level.
2. Do not overfill the transmission.
3. Check all fan belts for wear, cracks and fraying.
4. Have your car tuned up every 12,000 miles.
5. Check the battery periodically.
6. Check all hoses for softness and for cracks.
7. Check the tires regularly.
8. Have all accessories off when starting the car or they will put an extra drain on the battery.
9. Check the shock absorbers periodically.
10. Check the exhaust system for holes, leaks or loose fittings.

In my opinion, 90% of breakdowns on the road could be avoided by preventive maintenance. The concept of preventive maintenance or checking and repairing before the vehicle breaks down was pioneered and is practiced by government agencies, taxi companies and all large auto, truck and bus fleets. They realize that any time and money spent preventing problems before they occur will be cheaper than having the vehicle towed home or having it repaired elsewhere. Take my word for it: preventive maintenance is cheaper and less troublesome than repairs. In addition, work that may have to be done will be indicated in advance and be less of a shock to your budget than having it done while on a vacation or right after Christmas.

If you think about this, you will realize that two minutes spent checking the air in your spare tire will be nothing compared to finding that it is flat while standing along some turnpike in mid-February, having to wait for a tow truck and, possibly, buying a new tire at scalper prices from a turnpike gas station.

Have the brakes checked periodically. It's better to find out in advance if there is anything wrong.

Taking A Trip

If you haven't checked and tuned your car on a regular schedule all year, a good time to do it finally is before taking a trip. Plan to take it in for a checkup, or do it yourself, well before departing so that if something needs repair, time will be available. Quick checks are bad as there is always a greater possibility of missing something important. With a complete checkup, you can be reasonably sure of a safe trip.

If you haven't had a tune-up within, say, 10,000–12,000 miles, this is the time to do it or have it done. Definitely check such things as: oil (when was it last changed?), brakes, front end alignment, tires, cooling system and windshield wipers.

Also before departure it would be smart to put the following spares in your trunk: fan belts, fuses, points, epoxy cement, a one quart can of oil and, of course, the regular additional tools mentioned earlier in Chapter Two, in the section titled Tools.

Should you be contemplating towing a trailer, whether it be a house trailer, camper trailer or luggage hauler, make doubly sure the towing apparatus is secure and check it frequently. If you do not normally tow a trailer, you will have to have the trailer lights connected to your car's taillights and brake lights as this is required in most states.

If you have a car-top carrier, double check its security and also check it frequently while on the road. Be especially mindful of any driving regulations and speed limits that might be different from your own state and that change from state to state and in other countries.

How To Operate A Clutch

For quite a few years now, most American cars sold have had automatic transmissions. However, many foreign cars only offer standard transmissions and increasing numbers of domestic cars come equipped with four speed standard transmissions. A standard transmission gives the driver a little more control of the car and traditionally is more economical than the automatic. For those of you who learned to drive on an automatic car and have never had the opportunity to drive a standard, I'll give you an introductory lesson on how to operate the clutch. If you are planning to buy a car, don't immediately dismiss the standard or "stick" shift. Often they are cheaper on new cars and will contribute to better gas mileage.

Of course, there is no substitute for on the road practice but some basic theory before taking to the road will be helpful.

As I explain in Chapter Five, the automobile engine produces power which is transferred to the transmission and, ultimately, to the rear wheels. There are times, however, when this power should *not* be transferred to the transmission such as when idling, parking, and when shifting gears. The function of a clutch is to disengage the power of the engine from the transmission. When the clutch is pushed in, the turning engine is disconnected from the transmission, allowing the car to idle without moving or allowing the gears to be shifted without grinding. With an automatic transmission this disengagement is done automatically.

We don't have to get into a complicated discussion of the intricate mechanics and theory of clutch operation, it is sufficient to suggest that you keep in mind the fact that the engine is always turning when the car is running. Therefore, you should *always* start a standard transmission car in Neutral.

Gear Positions

All standard transmissions have what is called an "H" shift pattern. When learning to drive a stick shift, visualize this H in your mind. If the car has a three speed transmission, the upper left position on the H is Reverse; the bottom left position is First; the upper right position is Second; and the lower right position is Third. The middle part of the H is Neutral.

If the car has a four speed transmission, this same H pattern is used but there is also a leg off to one side for Reverse. So, the upper left position is First; the lower left position is Second; the upper right position is Third; and the lower right position is Fourth. Reverse will be farther to either side and up or down depending on the car. Neutral will be the middle position of the H.

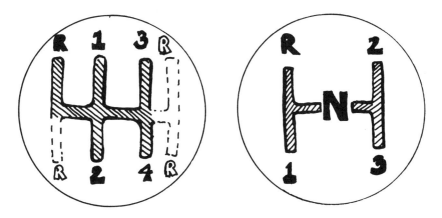

The "H" shift pattern.

Now that you know where the gears are and where to put the shifter, let's try to drive it. Start the car in Neutral (without using the clutch) and let it warm up to reduce the chances of stalling. Try the clutch, with your left foot, a few times without taking the shifter out of Neutral. This will give you the feel of the pressure and give you a chance to sense what is called the "grab point." Remember, in Neutral the engine is turning and so is the transmission. When you depress the clutch pedal, the engine keeps turning but the transmission stops turning. At about 1/3 of the way down on the clutch pedal, you will feel this "grab point" where the engine and transmission connect and disconnect.

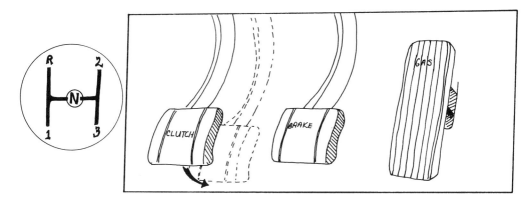

Put the clutch in and shift from Neutral to First.

Starting Out

Let's try it for real—usually a deserted parking lot or back road is the best place to learn. Push the clutch in with your left foot and, keeping it all the way in, put the shifter in the First gear position. The trick here is to let the transmission *slowly* pick up the engine's power.

You must now do two things at once: *slowly* let the clutch pedal out and *slowly* depress the gas pedal at the same time. Don't forget that the sudden requirement on the engine to also turn the transmission will demand increased engine power. So when you reach that "grab point" 2/3 of the way up on the pedal, you will have to be giving the engine enough gas to provide that increased power.

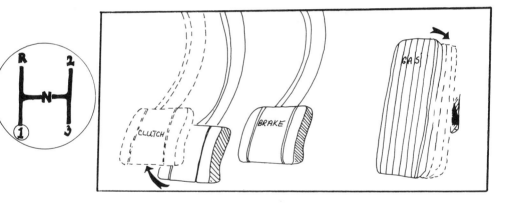

Ease the clutch out and ease the gas pedal down.

As you let the clutch all the way out and gradually accelerate the engine, you will hear the engine go faster and work harder. This is your cue to shift from First into Second. To do this, push in the clutch and simultaneously take your right foot off of the gas pedal. While both of your feet are occupied with the pedals, use your right hand to bring the shifter around the H into Second gear and then let the clutch out while accelerating the gas pedal again. Then use the same technique to shift from Second gear into Third and then into Fourth.

When you slow down to stop or go up a hill, you will need to "downshift" the gears and the same clutch pedal/gas pedal coordination technique applies. Simply push in the clutch pedal while letting off the gas pedal and take the shifter from Fourth into Third, Third into Second, etc., letting the clutch pedal back out in between shifts and pushing the clutch in when you are just about to come to a stop.

As usual, practice makes perfect and, for some drivers, learning to use your right foot on the brake pedal instead of your left which is now occupied with the clutch, will be an additional task.

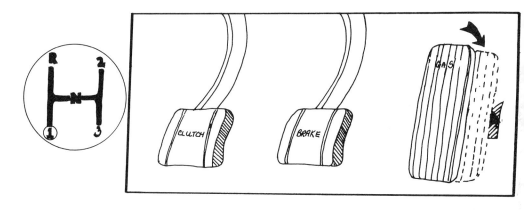

Accelerate in First with your foot completely off the clutch.

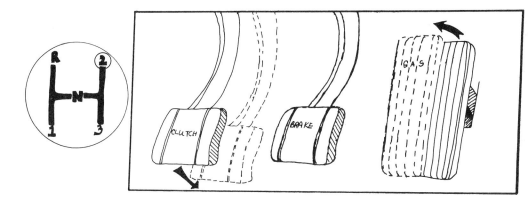

To shift into Second, let your right foot off the gas pedal, push the clutch in with your left foot and shift from First to Second.

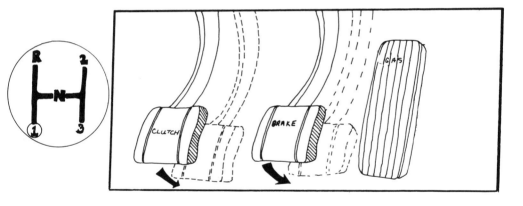

Let the clutch back out slowly while slowly accelerating again.

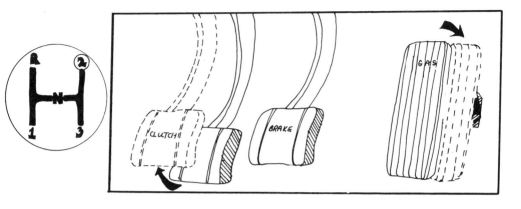

To stop, let off on the gas pedal and push in the clutch pedal. Then use your right foot to press the brake pedal.

Chapter 4

What's That Thing?

As all you women know or suspect, a car is made up of hundreds of complex gadgets; but we should find out what they are, generally what they are used for and where they are, so the car will work for us and not against us when trouble arises.

The Dashboard: Lights And Gauges

Good pilots start by familiarizing themselves with the instrument panel. Similarly, a car's dashboard contains various gauges and indicators which warn you if your car isn't functioning properly in regard to temperature, oil, gas and electricity. Now this can become complicated as all cars purposely have different instrument arrangements to distinguish them from the competition; some cars have gauges and some have "idiot lights." Idiot lights are usually red and they come on when something is wrong. When the red lights come on, it doesn't mean Christmas—it usually means trouble. The motor trade calls them idiot lights because they provide a signal to someone who is too much of an idiot to be able to read gauges. However, I call them idiot lights because you are an idiot if you don't pull over and shut the car off when they come on.

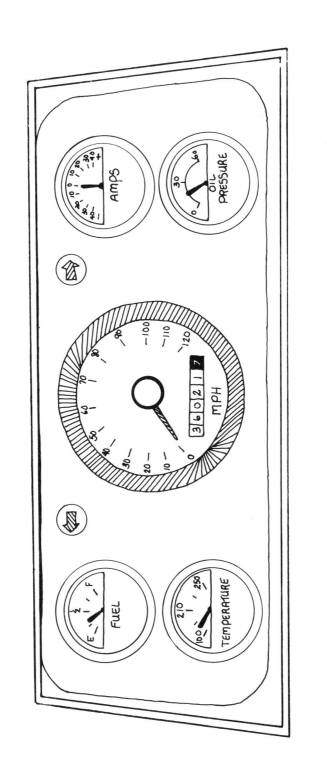

Once in a while there will be a malfunction in the light or gauge itself, in which case you can continue driving without hurting anything. But this is a risk unless you know for sure—so stop and shut off the engine.

Oil Light Or Oil Pressure Gauge

When the red oil light comes on or when the needle drops on the oil pressure gauge, it is a sign that there is no oil or that the oil is not going where it should. This can be extremely serious so stop immediately and find the cause for the warning.

Temperature Light or Gauge

If the temperature light comes on or the temperature gauge goes way up, it means that there is not enough water in the cooling system or that a leak has caused the water to boil. In either case shut the engine off and locate the problem or call the garage.

Alternator Light or Ammeter Gauge

Often, this will be a green light or a gauge marked "battery" or "amps." If it is a gauge, the needle will normally stay right in the middle of a range from "Charge" on one side to "Discharge" on the other end. If the light comes on or the needle heads toward "Discharge" or "—," it means that for some reason the alternator or generator is not recharging the battery as it should. The first thing to look for if this happens is a broken alternator drive belt. If you continue to drive without recharging the battery, it will soon deplete its electricity supply and you will have to stop. If the needle heads for the "Charge" or "+" side of the gauge, it is showing you that the alternator or generator is doing its job and recharging a taxed battery. However, this should only happen right after you start the car or after the battery has been drained or dead for some reason. If the needle is on "Charge" or "+" all the time, something else is wrong; possibly the votage regulator is not accurately regulating the amount of charge to the battery or perhaps the battery is not storing a charge for some reason. This situation also requires examination.

Gas Gauge

We all know this gauge well, especially nowadays. When this needle goes down, it only means one thing—out of gas. Look in your owner's manual for the size of your car's gas tank and then get to know your gas gauge. If, for example, the car has a twenty gallon tank, the gauge says it is half full and a "fill-up" requires twelve gallons, then your gas gauge is two gallons to the shy side. You should be very familiar with what the gauge indication means in terms of gallons left in the tank, especially when deciding how soon you must stop for gas.

Heed The Warning

I have seen too many cases where people have pulled into a garage with the bearings knocking or boiling water flying out and the car near ruin. I ask: "Didn't you see the red light come on?" to which comes the reply: "Oh, yes. But it kept running so I made it in." Little did they know that a lot of damage was probably already done.

It's like the man going the wrong way on a one-way street. The officer stopped him and said: "Didn't you see the arrows?" and the driver answered: "What arrows? I didn't even see the Indians."

So pay attention, girls, and watch the danger signals.

The Engine

Upon raising the hood, or "bonnet" on foreign cars, you will see a massive hunk of iron covered with hoses, wires and gadgets; it looks like a big mess at first but throughout this chapter these gadgets will be identified and become understandable and familiar to you.

Every engine is equipped with one or two cylinder heads, depending on whether it has four, six or eight cylinders. If it is a four or six cylinder engine, it has a gadget on the side with long tubes coming out of it. This is really two things: an intake manifold and an exhaust manifold. If the car has an eight cylinder engine, there is one exhaust manifold on each side and one intake manifold on the top center of the engine.

On the very bottom of the engine an oil pan is mounted and this holds the oil that lubricates the engine and thereby prevents it from wearing out. When the engine is filled with oil, it all goes down into this oil pan; then when the engine is running, a small

Your first impression when lifting the hood.

pump in the oil pan sends the oil up into the engine to circulate around the moving parts and keep them slick and oily so that metal will not rub against metal which causes rapid wear.

The oil in the engine gets very dirty after about 3,000 miles from picking up all the dirt and carbon particles within the engine (which is one of the other things circulating oil is designed to do), so every 3,000 miles you should have your gas station or garage drain out the old, dirty oil and replace it with fresh, clean oil so that your car's engine will stay continuously clean. This is very important and very inexpensive maintenance because the engine's greatest enemy is dirt and sludge. A dirty, worn-out engine will run less smoothly and efficiently and therefore get worse gas mileage, among other things.

So be very conscientious about having your oil changed every 3,000 miles. In a later chapter I will tell you how to easily change the oil yourself.

As the oil is pumped up from the oil pan into the working parts of the engine, it goes through an oil filter. This filter is mounted on the outside of the engine, usually on the side, and it is a small canister—about the size of a tin can. As its name suggests, it filters

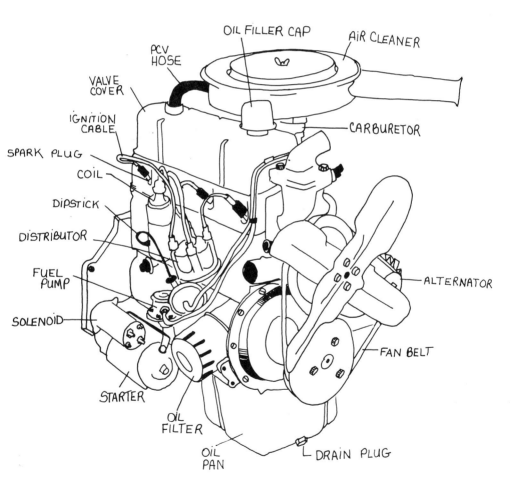

A four cylinder engine—count the spark plugs.

the junk out of the oil but after about 3,000 miles it fills to capacity with impurities. A new one costs about $2.00 and should *always* be replaced when the oil is changed. An oil filter holds about a quart of dirty oil so if you change the oil and don't change the filter, you

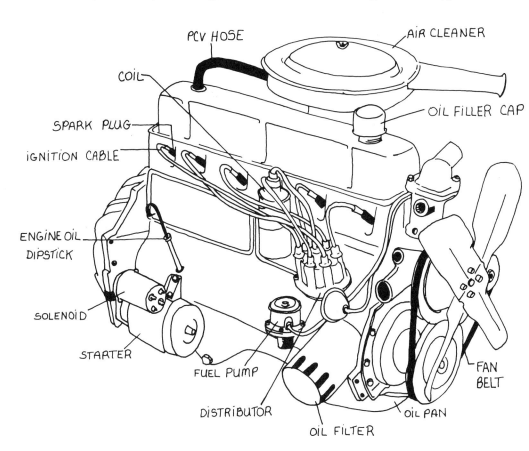

A six cylinder engine.

are already contaminating the new oil with the quart of dirty oil left in the filter. Besides, isn't it fun to think of the images you are shattering when you calmly ask at the garage if the oil filter has *also* been changed (that's assuming that this time you were a little too busy to handle it yourself)? Let's compare this engine to a heart. Without this diligent worker, you won't get too far. But, the gadgets attached to an engine or to a heart make it function. Take

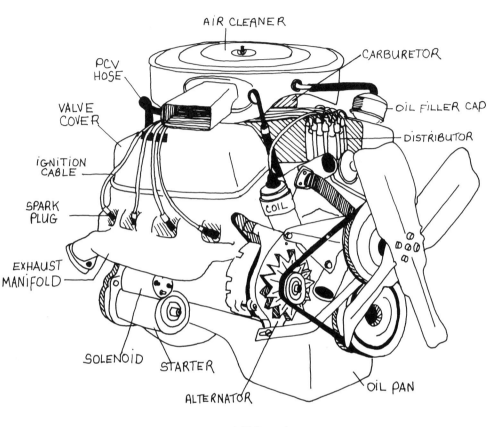

A V-8 engine.

those gadgets away and nothing will happen so let's get on to the gadgets and see what they do.

The engine, whether it is in the front or rear of the car, is supported by three mounts, two in the front and one at the rear. Between the engine and the mounts is a rubber cushion to absorb vibrations and noise.

Fan Belts

Considering their importance, fan belts rarely receive the attention they should. Does that sound familiar? All cars have at least one and some cars have two or three depending on such equipment as air conditioning, power steering, emission controls, etc. Belts resemble very large rubber bands, and they go around

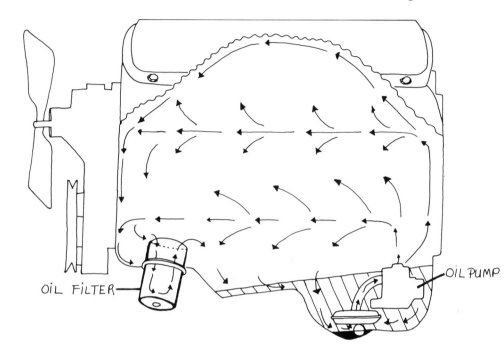

OIL FILTER

OIL PUMP

The oiling system in an engine. The oil is pumped from the pan up into the various parts of the engine, through a filter and back to the oil pan.

pulleys attached to the front of the engine. When the engine runs, it turns these pulleys which turn the belts which then operate these gadgets that I am about to describe to you. The belts must be kept tight and free from cracks and fraying.

The Alternator Or Generator

The first gadget to be discussed is called an alternator; on older cars it is called a generator. Either one is usually located on the right side (looking at the car from the front) and it is mounted on the front of the engine. It looks somewhat like a hair dryer with wires attached and is operated by one of the fan belts on the same principle as your vacuum cleaner. The difference is that the vacuum cleaner uses electricity to turn the belt which then turns the brushes. The alternator is turned by a belt which is driven by the engine; the alternator then produces electricity. This electricity is then sent to recharge the battery through the regulator.

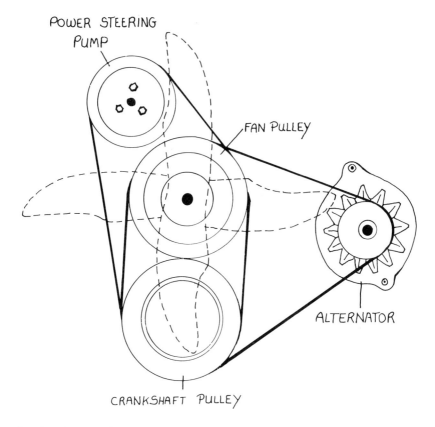

POWER STEERING PUMP

FAN PULLEY

ALTERNATOR

CRANKSHAFT PULLEY

The fan belts and pulleys. Only the crankshaft pulley turns by itself—the connecting fan belts make the other pulleys turn.

The Regulator

The regulator is a small box, usually black or gray. It is mounted on the inside of the right or left fender or on the firewall (the wall between the engine and the passenger compartment). It has several small, colored wires pushed onto metal fingers on both sides and it is held down with two bolts. This little gem regulates the electricity so there is just enough to keep your battery fully charged at all times.

The battery calls for electricity; the alternator puts it out but cannot regulate how much goes to the battery. That's where the regulator comes in. If the alternator kept feeding the battery whether it needed it or not, it would burn up the battery. It's like lying in the sun: once you get a burn, it's asking for trouble to stay in the sun. If, for example, the battery keeps going dry (you *do* check it every time you get gas?) or the dash gauge shows that it is overcharging, you are being told that the regulator isn't doing its job.

The Battery

This is another item your car cannot do without. In most modern cars, the battery is under the hood and on the right or left side in plain view. On some foreign cars it is found under the back seat or in the trunk. It is an oblong or square black box with six colored caps across the top. On opposite ends of the top, cables are attached to posts which stick up from the battery about one inch. One is called the ground or negative cable and the other is called the positive cable and it goes to the starter. Where these cables attach to the battery (called terminals) should always be clean and tight.

The battery is the center of your car's electrical system: it produces and disperses all the electricity needed to operate your car and run the lights, radio and other devices. The approximate life span of a battery is two or three years if you regularly check the water level inside.

The Fuel System

You can hardly miss the item right on the top of your engine: it looks like a large saucer with a nut in the middle to hold it on. This is an air cleaner and it does just that: it filters the air going to the carburetor. Now, you are surely asking, what is a carburetor?

Carburetor

The carburetor sits right under the air cleaner and it looks like a pot with a butterfly flap in the center. It is usually brass or silver colored with a hose or two coming out of it and a lot of little arms and attachments covering the outside.

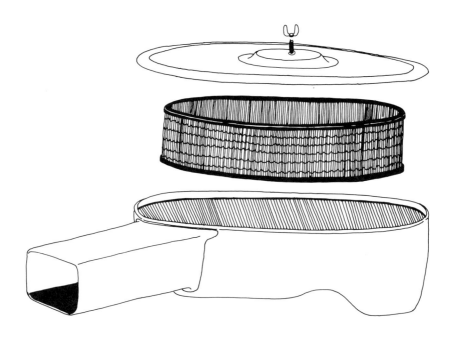

The air cleaner with the replaceable filter shown.

The carburetor is attached to the gas pedal inside your car. When you push the pedal down, the carburetor feeds the engine more gas and a mixture of air which makes the engine go faster. Your tank is filled with gas but the car doesn't run on gas alone, it has to be mixed with air and this is what the carburetor does. It gives a very particular gas and air mixture to the engine.

Where does the gas come from? A fuel pump, mounted on the engine, pumps gas from the tank which is located in the back, under the trunk. To find the fuel pump, follow the gas pipe from the carburetor down to the front or side of the engine; this pipe will end at the fuel pump.

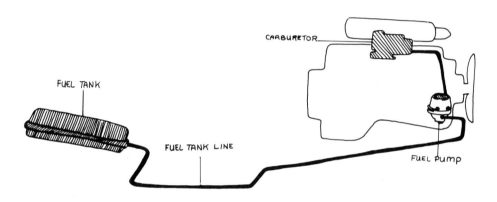

The fuel system.

The Ignition System

The ignition system of an engine is about the trickiest area of all but not impossible to master. So if we concentrate on the more obvious parts and aspects of the system, we should have no problem.

Distributor
Start first with the distributor. It looks like an octopus and it sticks right up out of the engine. If the car has an eight cylinder engine, the distributor will point straight up from the top front or back of the engine. If the car has a four or six cylinder engine, the distributor will slant up from the right side (facing forward). It will have a cluster of 5, 7 or 9 wires (one for each cylinder plus an extra)

coming out of a black plastic cap and running to the engine. These are called distributor wires or cables and each one goes from the distributor to a separate spark plug and the one extra middle wire goes to the coil.

The coil is mounted on the engine near the distributor and it looks like a big firecracker. Its function will be shown later.

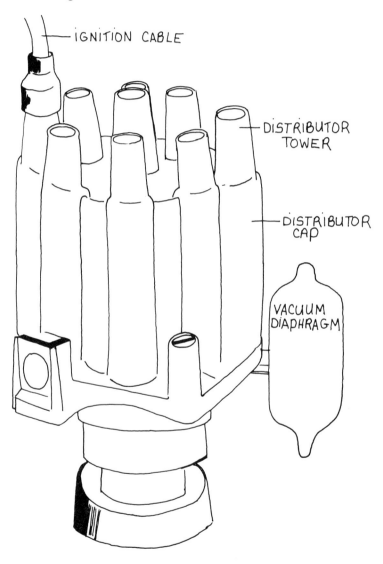

The distributor.

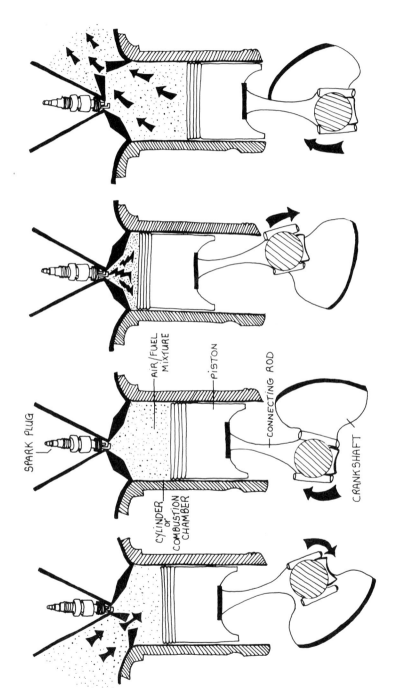

SPARK PLUG

AIR/FUEL MIXTURE

PISTON

CONNECTING ROD

CYLINDER or COMBUSTION CHAMBER

CRANKSHAFT

The sequence of events in one cylinder of an engine: 1) fuel and air enters, 2) the mixture is compressed by the piston, 3) the spark plug fires and ignites the mixture, 4) the piston is forced down which turns the crankshaft and leftover exhaust is let out.

You will remember that the carburetor mixes gas and air in the correct ratio. The spark plugs, to which the distributor wires are connected, are screwed into the engine at such an angle that this gas and air mixture passes by them. When it does, the coil and distributor send an electric charge through to the spark plugs. They, as you would imagine from their name, make a spark which ignites this gas/air mixture and causes an explosion. Thus the name "ignition system."

Because this explosion is confined inside a closed cylinder, it forces the bottom of the cylinder (actually the piston) to move downward. This turns a big crank inside the bottom of the engine. This turns a shaft attached to the transmission which then turns the driveshaft. The driveshaft causes the car's rear wheels to turn and thereby propel it down the road. Complicated? You bet.

Points

Inside the distributor are the points. Possibly you have heard that name because compared to many engine parts, these have shorter lives and are always replaced during a tune-up. The points look like a small set of snappers and they are very important because they break the electrical circuit at just the right instance to get the electricity to the correct spark plug.

If the points are burned, corroded or not timed properly, the car will not run smoothly and possibly will not start at all. Because they are subject to a great deal of heat and wear, they don't last forever. But replacement is not expensive and it will always improve the efficiency of your car.

We have now discussed, in simplified version, how the car runs, but we need a way of starting it. In the old days you could crank by hand, but not today. Ten men and a boy could not crank today's engines. If they managed *somehow*, the crank would kick back and throw them all sky-high. Even pushing the car to start it will not work unless you have a standard transmission. Because most cars now have an automatic transmission, pushing is also a remedy of the past.

The solution that evolved is the self-starter. Every car has one and it is located on the bottom rear of the engine and on either the left or the right side. To find it, follow the battery cables. One cable will attach to just a bolt on the engine—this is the ground cable and it grounds the electrical system.

The other battery cable goes to the starter. When you turn the ignition key to START, the starter (which is just a small high-speed electric motor) turns the engine fast enough for it to start. Now that the car starts and runs, let's make sure it will stop.

The Brakes

On the firewall (remember—the wall between the engine and the inside of the car) is mounted the brake master cylinder. It is usually round or oblong and has a cap held on by a screw or a clip. This master cylinder holds what is known as brake fluid. The master cylinder is like the heart of the braking system and the brake fluid running through the brake lines is just like the blood running through arteries and veins. Both are closed, pressurized systems which reuse their fluid. You can see the brake lines coming out of the bottom of the master cylinder. From there, they carry fluid to another cylinder in each wheel.

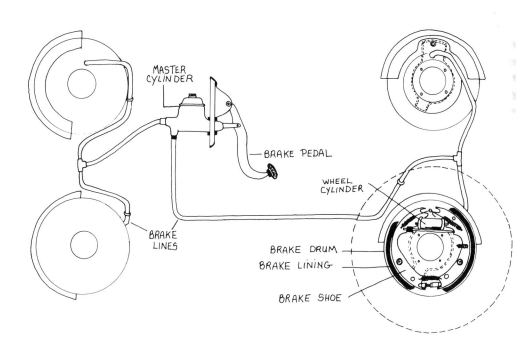

The brake system.

When you push the brake pedal down, it pushes a plunger inside the master cylinder which takes up all the room and thereby forces the fluid into the brake lines and through them to the cylinder at each wheel. The harder you press the pedal, the more pressure the master cylinder exerts on each wheel cylinder. This increased pressure causes the wheel cylinder to expand at both ends and force two asbestos pads (called linings) away from it. Remember, this is all going on inside each wheel. When these pads are forced away from the wheel cylinder, they rub against the inside surface of the wheel (commonly called the drum). This rubbing is so strong that it causes the wheels to stop turning which, naturally, stops the car.

If fluid leaks out of this normally closed system, no pressure can be created and the brakes will not work. Most modern cars have two separate systems: one for the rear wheels and one for the front wheels. This way if one leaks and fails, chances are good that the other will still be working and can stop the car. So look out for two separate master cylinders either next to each other or within one large tank.

Motorists aren't usually aware of the condition of their brakes. They will live with the same parts as long as they stop the car no matter how little pedal there is, not realizing that worn parts are extremely dangerous.

There is a good chance, when a car reaches 25,000 miles or more, that it will need new brake linings. But this depends on where and how you drive. When you do reline the brakes, it is always a good idea to overhaul the wheel cylinders because they can stick which would cause the new linings to wear down.

You can reduce the chance of accidents caused by brake failure if you check for visible leaks. Begin checking the fluid level by finding the master cylinder under the hood, removing its top and seeing the level. If the level is down, use only a good quality brake fluid (there are no substitutes) to restore the proper level.

When the pedal goes down farther than usual, something is wrong. Kneel down and look at the inside of each wheel. See if there is any sticky substance running down the wheel and, while in this position, have a look at the brake lines going to each wheel as they can also leak. In addition, check around the master cylinder for possible leaks.

The master cylinder is usually mounted on the left side of the firewall and if it isn't on the power brake unit, the rear of it will be exposed under the dashboard just above the steering column. Open the left front door and use a flashlight to find the point described. You will most likely see a sticky substance running down the inside of the firewall just above your brake pedal. You will also be able to smell its very strong alcohol type scent.

This is brake fluid and that's a master cylinder leak. If you sit at a light and hold your foot lightly on the pedal and it sinks to the floor, this is also a sign of a leak somewhere. If you then check the brake fluid in the master cylinder and find it full, then you have a bad master cylinder. Although the fluid leak may not show, it is there. The fluid is bypassing the front cup on the cylinder and is picked up by the rear cup so there is no loss of fluid but there is a loss of brake. A lot of mechanics are fooled by this but don't you be. The solution is to overhaul the cylinder or replace it which is much quicker and probably about the same price.

One word of caution: when putting brake fluid into the master cylinder, do not get it on the car's paint or it will take it off just like paint remover.

Disc Brakes

Most foreign cars come equipped with disc brakes on all four wheels and many American cars come with disc brakes on the front wheels and drum brakes on the rear wheels. Disc brake systems, like drum brake systems, have a master cylinder and brake lines and they use the same pressure principle. But instead of brake shoes, linings and drums, there is a brake pad, a caliper and a rotor (or disc). When you push the brake pedal the fluid in the master cylinder is forced through the brake lines and into the caliper. This pressure causes two pads to be forced toward each other from about an inch apart. When they are squeezed in this manner, they pinch the spinning rotor which is attached to the wheel. The whole process is much like pinching a spinning phonograph record between your fingers to stop it. When the pads pinch the rotor like this, they effectively stop the wheels from turning and therefore the car from moving. But, like drum brake linings, disc brake pads wear and must be checked twice a year and replaced if worn so they won't score the rotor.

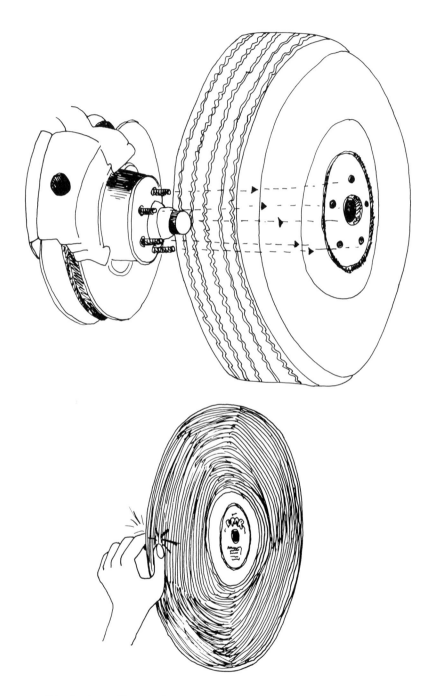

Disc brakes—like pinching a spinning record with your fingers.

The Cooling System

Ninety percent of today's cars are cooled by water. Volks-
wagen and Corvair are the two notable exceptions to this rule and
they are air cooled. On an air cooled engine the built-up heat is
dissipated by designing the engine so that air drawn in by the
cooling fan can circulate all around the hot parts of the engine and
cool it down.

Water Pump

The water pump is mounted right behind the fan. As the fan
belt turns the fan pulley, it also turns the water pump. This
fan/water pump combination is mounted on the upper front of
the engine and looks much like any home fan. Just like the fan at
home, keep your hands, clothes and long hair away from it. It runs
so fast that you can't even see the blades.

The main function of the water pump is to circulate water
through the whole engine to keep the internal parts from heating
beyond a certain temperature.

The Radiator

If you face your car with the hood open, the first object in
sight, right behind the grille, is a large square honeycombed article
with a tank across the top and a cap on top of that. This is the
radiator. The fan and water pump I mentioned earlier are located
in the front of the engine but several inches behind the radiator.

The radiator is filled with water and antifreeze. Needless to
say, as the engine heats up and this water is circulated through it,
the water itself becomes quite hot. So never open the cap of the
radiator unless the engine is completely cold or else the combination of 200° water and great pressure will knock you over and
severely burn you.

The water in the radiator is circulated through the engine via
two connecting hoses. One is the lower hose and this carries water
from the radiator through the water pump and into the engine.
The circulated water returns to the radiator via the upper
connecting hose.

The fan blades suck air in through the radiator and this cool air
goes around the little water pipes which are inside the radiator.

This cools the water so it can go back into the engine through the hose at the bottom of the radiator. The cycle is continuous: the water is constantly being cooled in the radiator, running through the engine to cool it off and then, being reheated by that job, it goes back through the radiator to be cooled and start all over again.

Thermostat

The only restriction in this cooling circulation process is the thermostat. It is normally located in the top of the engine where the upper radiator hose enters the engine. When the engine is cold, the thermostat is closed and it restricts water circulation. When the engine warms up, the thermostat opens and lets the water circulate freely. The thermostat warms up quickly because all engines and heaters operate better when the engine is warm— just like people and houses!

Hoses

The two radiator hoses are not the only hoses to be seen under the hood of your car. In addition, there are heater hoses which run from the engine back through the firewall, diverting some of the hot water to the heater and defroster inside the car. A heater and a radiator may be the same at home but not in your car, so don't get confused.

There may also be air conditioning hoses which run from the air conditioning compressor attached to the engine back into the passenger compartment of the car.

Another very visible hose is one which runs from one of the cylinder heads back into the intake manifold. This is the crankcase ventilation hose and it sends some of the gases left over from combustion back into the cylinders for another try at being burned with the fuel. This is one of the basic parts of your car's emission control system and a device called a PCV valve is contained in one end of this hose. PCV stands for Positive Crankcase Ventilation and it is sort of a safety valve so the gases can only go in one direction: back into the cylinders.

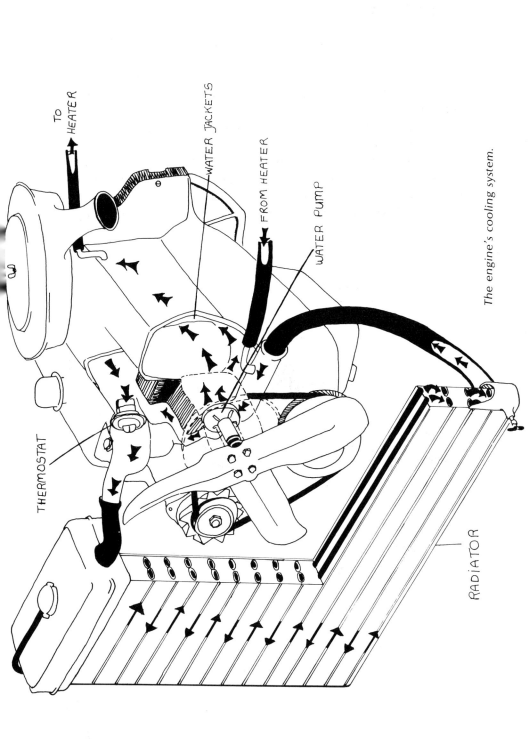

TO HEATER

WATER JACKETS

FROM HEATER

WATER PUMP

THERMOSTAT

RADIATOR

The engine's cooling system.

Power Steering

Most noncompact new cars come equipped with power steering. This requires another one of those drive belts I mentioned. The belt drives a steering pump which resembles a large pot with a lid on top. It is located on the front of the engine and it has a small wheel on it as does the alternator. This wheel is called a pulley and the drive belt hooks over this pulley and turns the steering pump.

This pump feeds oil to the steering box through two rubber hoses. If you wish to find the steering box, follow these two hoses right to it. If your car has power steering and begins to steer hard, look for a broken drive belt or low oil in the steering pump.

With power steering, today's cars are beautiful to steer and park. The old cars didn't have this ease of steering but they also didn't have the power steering equipment to maintain and repair such as the pump, gears and hoses.

If you remember where the power steering pump is located— usually on the left front of the engine—look for a dipstick in the pump which you can pull out and check. It will say something like "Full" and "Add Oil." If it is below or on "Add Oil," then add some automatic transmission fluid (ATF).

If the pump has a leak, it will often be found behind the pulley or at the reservoir where you put the oil in. Next check the two rubber hoses going into the pump: one is the pressure hose and the other is the return line. It is usually the pressure hose that leaks. Follow the hose down to the steering box. This box can leak at several points but the most common spot is where the cross-shaft comes out at the bottom of the box.

Suspension and Underbody

If you could tip your car over on its side or, more realistically, study it while it is up on a lift at the garage, figuring out what all the components are and what they do would be quite a job. However, with a short introductory course here, you can prepare yourself for actually seeing what is underneath the car.

Three major systems are housed under there and they are: the suspension system, the drive train and the exhaust system.

Suspension
Front   Almost all cars use coil springs to suspend the front of the vehicle. These springs are attached to the frame of the car at their top and to the front axle at their bottom; they accomplish several tasks. They put a little distance between you and the bumps in the road; they make the car ride evenly despite the unevenness of the road and they let the tires, wheels and axle take the abuse of bumps rather than the whole car. Springs usually last for the life of the average car but if your car has a great deal of mileage under its belt, chances are good that the springs have sagged and should be replaced.

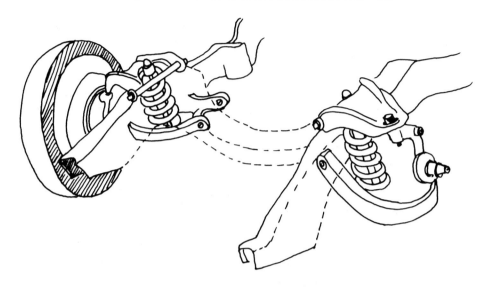

The front coil springs.

Rear   Most cars use leaf springs to suspend the rear of the vehicle. Leaf springs may not be at all familiar to you because, unlike coil springs, they do not look like the common spring. Leaf springs are "U" shaped and the bottom of the U is attached under the rear axle. The top sides of this U are spread apart and each one is attached to the frame of the car. One end is attached to the car in front of the rear axle and the other end is attached behind the rear axle. Cars usually leaf springs at the rear have two: one spring for each side of the rear axle. As the rear wheels and axle go over a bump, they push the spring upward and the spring, after contracting, will then force the axle back down to where it should be.

Front and Rear   If cars used only springs, the vehicle would be constantly bouncing up and down to every bump and irregularity in the road. To compensate for this, shock absorbers are used. Like springs, they are attached to the axles and to the frame, front and rear, and there are also four of them—one at each corner of the car. Shocks, as they are commonly called, are double acting which means that they take the bump when the car rises as well as when it comes down. If, by comparison, you bounce a baby carriage once or twice, it will continue to bounce after you stop

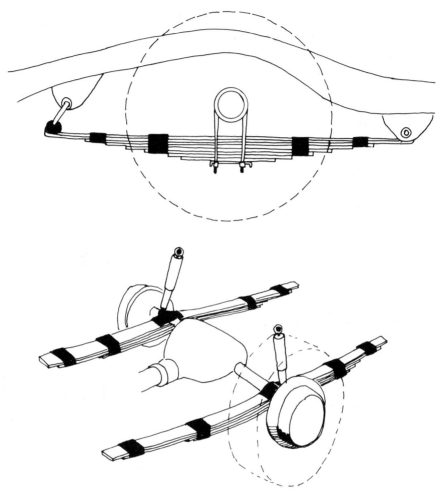

The rear leaf springs.

A Shock absorber—two in front and two in the rear.

causing it to because it has no shock absorbers. But with shock absorbers, a car bounces up once then comes down and stops. Aside from giving the passengers a more comfortable ride, shock absorbers make steering easier by keeping the motion of the car under control.

The Drive Train

The drive train is what connects the engine to the rear wheels and transmits the power created by the engine to making the car move. Contained in the drive train are the transmission, the drive-shaft, the differential and the rear axle.

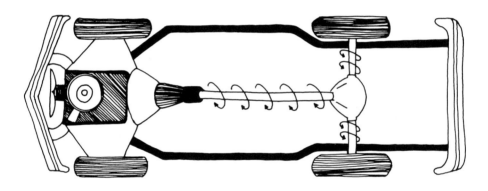

The drive train—engine, transmission, driveshaft, differential and rear axle.

The Transmission

The transmission, whether an automatic or a standard, is connected to the back of the engine. It, too, has a pan mounted on the bottom which holds transmission fluid. Because the transmission is sealed from outside exposure (unlike the engine which needs outside air to run), very little dirt can get into the transmission fluid. However, the transmission gets very hot during operation and this will eventually have an effect on the composition of the fluid. This fluid should be changed every 30,000 or 40,000 miles but on newer cars this is not as critical.

The transmission transfers power from the engine to the rear axle and then to the rear wheels which push the car along. The transmission contains a lot of gears which, when shifted into different combinations by you or automatically, make the engine's power usable or applicable to specific situations like backing up, driving up a hill, slowing down or cruising on the turnpike.

Connecting the back of the transmission to the differential in the middle of the rear axle is the driveshaft. The engine turns the transmission gears, they turn the driveshaft and the driveshaft (through additional gears in the differential) turns the rear axle. The back wheels are bolted onto the rear axle so they turn when the axle turns. When you get an "oil change and lube" at your service station, the mechanic also checks the level of gear oil in the differential so this is one more reason to have your car serviced regularly.

Exhaust System

Still looking at the bottom of the car, you will see a big pipe running from the engine all the way to the back of the car. Some-where along this pipe, usually near the middle or rear of the car, is the muffler. Some cars, particularly larger or high performance cars, have two pipes and two mufflers—one on each side of the underneath.

This is the engine's exhaust system and it is the method by which the excess gases and leftovers are expelled from the engine after that internal explosion we discussed (called combustion).

It is absolutely imperative that this system be kept tightly sealed because if these gases escape underneath the car, they can

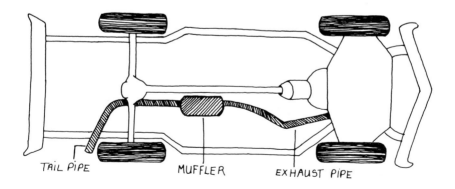

TAIL PIPE   MUFFLER   EXHAUST PIPE

The exhaust system.

easily be drawn up into the passenger compartment and poison you. Carbon monoxide, which is in the exhaust, is especially deadly because while it is poisoning you its odor is undetectable . . . you just fall quietly asleep. Each year many people die from carbon monoxide poisoning and the reason is usually a leaky exhaust system which permits gases to seep up into the passenger compartment. Symptoms are dizziness, headache and nausea. Too often people know these signs but go on driving probably diagnosing it as car sickness.

Detecting faulty exhaust systems is another purpose of the state inspection system. If you live in a state that does not have a thorough inspection program, it would pay you to have these details checked or check them yourself. A few points to do are:

1. Check your car for holes in the floor and body.

2. Check the exhaust system thoroughly for holes and leaks.

3. Do not sit with the engine running for more than a few minutes.

4. Do not run the car in a closed garage.

5. If you notice a strange smell in the car, have the system checked right away. The smell would be exhaust for carbon monoxide is odorless.

6. If you feel nauseous, dizzy or headachey, pull to the side of the road and get out into the fresh air.

Visible Exhaust Problems

This assignment is a little difficult unless the car is up in the air or something is visibly dragging so the best time to check the system is when the car is up on a lift and you can walk around underneath it. Don't be afraid—very few mechanics have been crushed by falling cars. Start back at the tailpipe end looking for holes as you work your way forward. Check all connections between the muffler and pipes and where the front pipe connects to the engine. You can tell if there are leaks at any point because a black, sooty mark will be made on the exhaust pipe. Do not be alarmed at rust on the system because the surface rusts almost as soon as the car goes outside due to water and salt on the roads. Be especially watchful for holes on the top, hidden part of the pipe. They will allow fumes—which often escape notice—to go up into the car.

While looking under the car, check all brackets and clamps that support the exhaust system. If these are broken, part or all of the system can fall on the ground. But don't be alarmed if the whole system shakes a bit because it is hung in rubber and shakes with the engine.

Mufflers and tailpipes rot out from condensation (caused by hot engine by-products) which lies in the mufflers and pipes. Short trips are particularly conducive to this as the exhaust hardly has a chance to dry it out so the water just stays there and eats away at the metal.

The Gas Tank

Before we leave the underbody of the car, take a look at the gas tank. It's that large, flat rectangular pan at the extreme rear of the car. It is held in place by two metal straps and a quick look will show whether they are in good condition. I cannot elaborate too much on the dangers of leaking gasoline which, we all know, is highly explosive.

A gasoline odor should be the first sign of a leak somewhere in the system. Whether the leak is around the carburetor, fuel pump or tank, locate it immediately and have it fixed. An ignition spark or gas leaking on a hot exhaust manifold can cause a fire and possibly an explosion so don't drive a car which is leaking gas somewhere.

While on the subject of gasoline, don't think the gas station attendant is doing you a favor by squeezing every possibly drop into your tank. On a hot day gasoline will expand and run out the overflow pipe or cap. Aside from this raw gasoline being very flammable, the fumes in the atmosphere are also a prime source of air pollution (hydrocarbons). Late model cars have a sealed fuel system which forces gas overflow into a return pipe and back into the gas tank.

One last piece of advice concerning gasoline: don't carry extra gas in cans in the trunk of your car, particularly if driving any distance. The resultant fumes, spills, and great danger of explosion from heat or impact make carrying a few gallons of gas hardly worth the risk. There have been too many news articles lately about people being burned or killed trying to beat the gasoline shortage. Five or ten gallons of gas is not worth your life.

Emission Controls

Air pollution and emission control systems are probably not new words to you but what they actually mean may be another story. Most air pollution, or smog, is caused by large concentrations of automobiles emitting pollutants into the atmosphere. There are three types of pollutants created by an automobile engine: carbon monoxide which I have already mentioned, hydrocarbons and oxides of nitrogen.

The amount of carbon monoxide emitted into the air can be controlled by adjusting the air/fuel mixture created in the carburetor so that there is less fuel or a "leaner" mixture.

Hydrocarbons are a product of the raw gasoline that is left unburned after combustion in the engine. If the modern engine were efficient enough to completely burn all the gasoline, there would be no hydrocarbons in the air. Because this level of efficiency has not been reached, the amount of hydrocarbons emitted has been somewhat controlled by reburning them as they come out of the cylinder through the exhaust manifold.

One of the effects of attempts to control automotive emissions has been engines that run much hotter than in the pre-emission era. This has inadvertently caused an increase in the emission of oxides of nitrogen which appear in quantity only when combustion temperatures rise above a certain level—a heat level which had been uncommon before emission-controlled engines.

Unfortunately, the emission of oxides of nitrogen are more difficult to control than the others and they are also more dangerous. In order to contain emissions as much as possible and as soon as possible, auto makers have designed add-on gadgets for engines already in existence and such gadgets have lessened gas mileage, made cars run less smoothly and made it more difficult to tune an engine accurately.

For you, as a potential do-it-yourself mechanic, emission-controlled engines make the job more difficult. Often special testing equipment is required to achieve the exact settings necessary for this equipment to function properly. Furthermore, the presence of this equipment and its possible adverse effects on mileage and driveability require more frequent and more accurate tune-ups.

So it is that much more imperative that your car be tuned up on a regular basis, preferably every 10,000–12,000 miles.

Air Conditioning

What a wonderful gadget the car air conditioner is. If your car is equipped with one, you'll find that it is the largest component driven by a belt from the engine. It is always at the front of the

engine on the upper right or left. This is the compressor and hoses run from it back through the firewall and into the passenger compartment.

Generally the automotive mechanic is not also equipped to repair air conditioning which is a field of its own. But a huge percentage of new cars have air conditioning so they are usually repaired by specialty shops which are often quite expensive.

An automotive air conditioner can leak gases (freon) just as your refrigerator or home air conditioner can, and it is odorless. The only way to detect a leak is an annual checkup. Things you can do are keep anti freeze in the cooling system all year round and check the operation of the system every so often. Take a look at the compressor and you will see a small glass-covered hole. This is the sight glass and the presence of bubbles in the liquid within it usually means there is a leak; but the engine and the air conditioner must be running for the bubbles to be visible. While inspecting the air conditioner and its sight glass, be careful of the fan and belts.

Chapter 5

What You Can Check Yourself

Engine Oil

Now that you know where and what the gadgets are, let's try to *do* some things for yourself.

First, the engine oil level should be checked between oil changes and chassis lubrications. As far as I am concerned, the oil level should be checked every 300–500 miles. The dipstick can be found on the right or left side of the engine, near the front. The oil level can be checked hot or cold but the engine must be turned off. Pull the dipstick out of the engine, wipe it off with a rag or paper towel, stick it back in all the way and leave it there for a few seconds. Then pull it out again and read it. If the engine is cold, the level should be a little over the mark that reads "Full." If the engine is warm, the level should be between the "Full" and "Add Oil" marks. Of course, if the level is at the "Add Oil" mark, add one quart.

Be careful, when anyone else checks it for you, to make sure that the dipstick is all the way in or you will be sold a quart of oil

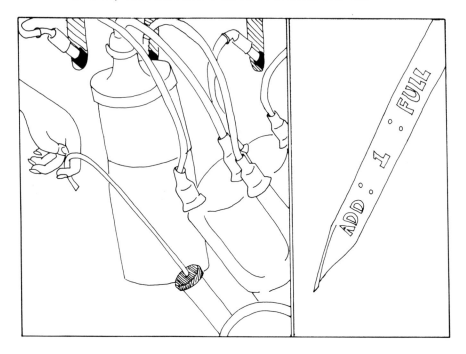

Checking the engine oil level. Reading the dipstick.

you don't need. Don't be afraid to watch them check the oil and ask to see the reading. After all, careful consumer shopping is what this book is about.

Transmission Fluid

To check the transmission fluid level, start the car in Park or Neutral with the emergency brake on. The transmission dipstick is located under the hood on the right or left side, near the lower rear of the engine. As before, pull it out, wipe it off, reinsert it and draw it out again to read the oil level.

If the level is at the "Add Oil" mark, add one quart at a time using only specially marked automatic transmission fluid. ATF, as it is commonly called, has a special consistency to withstand great heat and to prevent it from foaming or bubbling. Do not overfill the transmission as the fluid will only leak out or break the transmission seals.

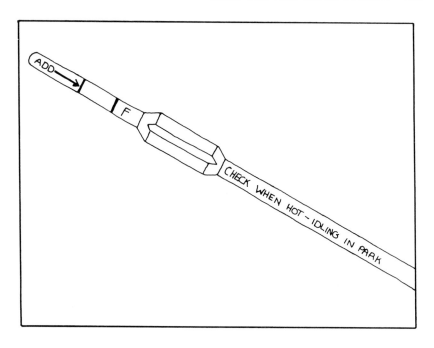

The transmission fluid dipstick.

Cooling System Level

The level of water or coolant in the radiator must also be checked regularly but, as I keep telling you, do not remove the cap when it is hot. Wait until everything has cooled and then remove the cap to check the level and add water or antifreeze as necessary. Do not fill it to the very top as it will just go out the overflow tube onto the ground. On most late model cars, it will say "FILL TO HERE" right inside the radiator filler neck.

Some late model cars also have an expansion tank; combined with the radiator this is called a "sealed system." Such systems have a white plastic jug on the right or left side of the radiator with two rubber hoses running to it from the overflow tube on the radiator. It is clearly marked and provides a receptacle for the cooling system water to overflow into when heat and pressure build up in the system. When the system cools down again, the water that overflowed can then return to the radiator.

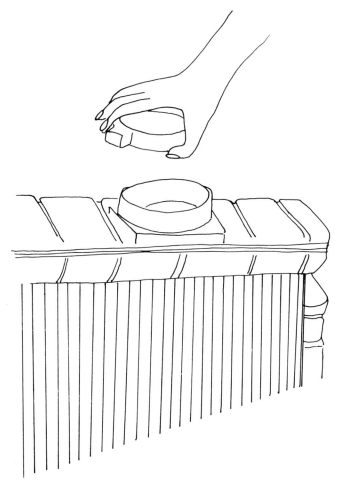

Checking the radiator level.

Do not confuse this expansion tank with the window washer bottle which is smaller, usually nearer to the firewall and connected to squirter jets on the hood or cowl. With a sealed cooling system, you never need to remove the radiator cap; any water or antifreeze to be added goes right into the expansion tank.

While checking the radiator level, look at the bottom of the radiator and at the hose connections for stains or any other visible signs of leaks.

Battery Level

Batteries normally require water at least once a month. Remove the battery caps and look down into the holes; part way down each hole you will see a circle. Add water up to that circle but not above it.

Power Steering Fluid

The power steering pump, located on the front right or left side of the engine and driven by a fan belt, also has a small dipstick with which to check the fluid level. Turn this dipstick and pull it out. If the level is at "FULL," everything is O.K. If not, add enough automatic transmission fluid to bring the level up to "FULL." It is best that the power steering fluid level be checked while the engine is warm.

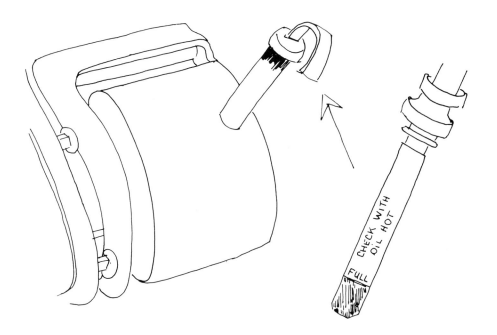

Checking the power steering fluid level.

Windshield Washer

The windshield washer fluid tank is mounted on the firewall or on the inside of the front left fender. It is smart to keep this bottle full in case of a sloppy day when you will need to wash the windshield often. In the summer you can fill it with water but for winter a quart of regular washer fluid keeps it from freezing in the bottle, melts the ice and cleans the windshield a little better than ordinary water.

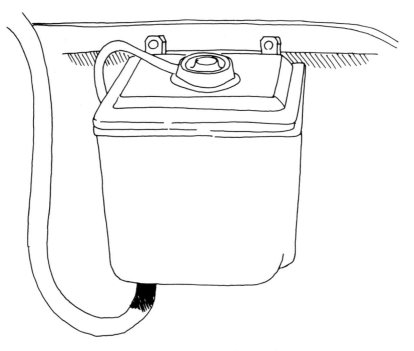

The windshield washer tank.

Tire Pressure

The air pressure in the tires is very important. To check it regularly you can buy and carry a portable tire pressure gauge or go to a garage. The pressure gauges at garages, which are usually part of the air pump, are notoriously unreliable and you would be smarter to invest a couple of dollars in your own gauge. The portable pressure gauge looks like a mechanical pencil and is about as easy to operate.

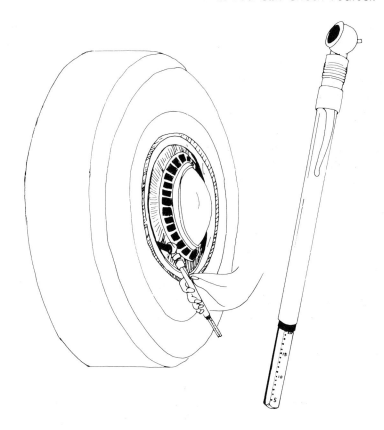

Checking the tire pressure with a pressure gauge.

Look on the tire for a little hose with a cap on the end coming out through the wheel and possibly through the wheel cover. Unscrew the small cap and you will see a pin in the middle of the little hose. If you place the round end of the tire gauge on the end of the little hose, the pin will be pushed in so that air can escape from the tire and into the gauge. This will push the other end of the gauge out just enough to show the tire's air pressure on the gauge's scale.

If the tire needs air, add some by placing the air hose right on the same end of the little hose. If the tire has too much air, release some by holding down the pin in the hose end while air escapes.

While checking the air pressure you should also check each tire for nails, cracks and irregular wearing which would indicate misalignment of the front end.

To make checking the tire treads much easier, start the car and turn the steering wheel all the way to one side. You will then be able to see most of the tread without having to bend way down. You can then turn the wheels all the way in the other direction to check the other sides.

Cupping or flat spots on the tire tread indicate that it is either out of balance, has bad shocks or has a loose front end. If one side of the tire is worn but the other isn't, there is probably a camber defect (an alignment term). A tire that is feathered out or in usually has toe-in problems (another alignment term).

Fan Belts

It would be a little difficult for most people to put on a new fan belt as several components must be loosened and moved, especially if the car has air conditioning. But with the engine OFF, you can simply turn the belts inside out as far as you can and inspect the inner surface for cracks and frays.

Chassis Lubrication

An oil change and lube job (chassis lubrication) should be done every 3,000 miles. If it goes longer without a lube, you will hear the chassis groan and squeak as you ride along. A regular lubrication keeps parts from sticking, binding, squeaking or even rusting and it provides you with a regular, easily followed maintenance schedule. When this is done at a gas station, they put a little sticker on the inside of the door noting the date and mileage so you will know when to do it again. If you get to the do-it-yourself stage where you change the oil and lubricate the car yourself, make sure you also keep track of the date and mileage.

Checking and Caring For Tires

It is very important, as I mentioned earlier, to check the tire pressure each week or two because even one underinflated tire can cause the car to sway and shimmy which will lead to front end misalignment and premature tire wear—not only on that tire but also on the other front tire. The sidewalls of an underinflated tire can easily break on sharp objects (as they also can on an overinflated tire). This is why the tire manufacturer recommends a particular tire pressure. They have tested their products and found what pressure is best under all conditions.

Wheel Balancing

Both front and rear wheels should be balanced—when new and every 10,000–15,000 miles thereafter. Balancing can be done in several ways but the basic idea is to have weight evenly distributed on the tire around the hub so that it spins on the axle with absolutely no wobble. In order to accomplish this, the wheel is spun on a machine with the tire mounted. The machine measures the weight distribution and indicates where any deficiencies are. The weight distribution is then made even by attaching small lead weights on the rim of the wheel until it is balanced or spins evenly. With balanced wheels on a car, most vibration and shimmy will be eliminated.

Retiring

The tires on your car are just as important as the shoes on your feet but, not having to match colors makes retiring a bit easier than buying new shoes. Tires are all black and white but, like shoes, they come in different sizes, materials and designs—not to mention prices. Due to steering design, wheel size, wheelbase, height, how you drive and how you like the car to drive and handle, a tire that works well on one car may not work well on another.

After deciding what size tire your car requires, you then must select the appropriate material and construction.

Tire Sizes

If you have ever shopped for tires, as opposed to the non-consumer method of just taking it to your gas station and asking for new ones, then you already know how terribly complicated the numbering system appears. Actually, understanding those numbers can give you a complete description of the size and design of a tire. Let's examine the numbers and find out what they mean. First, there are three types of number designations for tires that fit on the same car.

If a certain car came with a size 735-14 tire, the "735" means that the measurement from one sidewall through the tire to the other sidewall is 7.35 inches. The "14" means that the tire must be mounted on a wheel having a diameter of 14 inches. That may sound easy but that number only applies to bias ply type tires. If you chose to buy a belted bias ply tire for that same car (tire design will be discussed shortly), you would choose an E70–14 tire. In this designation, the "E" refers to that same 7.35 inch sidewall-to-sidewall measurement. The "70" means that the tire's road-to-rim height is 70% of its width. Remembering that the width is 7.35 inches, the height of the tire from the road to the bottom of the wheel rim is 5.15 inches or 70% of the 7.35 inch width. Again, the "14" refers to a 14 inch wheel diameter.

Now, if you choose to buy a radial tire for that same car, you would buy an ER70–14. The simple addition of the "R" identifies it as a radial design tire and the other numbers and letters mean the same as for a belted bias ply tire.

Often, tire charts will also show these designations in metric measurements. In that case, a radial tire for that same car would be a 205 R70–14. The "205" is simply 7.35 inches expressed in millimeters.

Simple? Well, not really. But you can get a head start by looking on the side of your car's tires. Whatever size and type it is will be stamped right there on the sidewall. Now that you know what your car has now, you can convert to any other type by using this conversion chart:

Tire Material and Types

The three tire types we will discuss are: bias ply, belted bias ply and belted radial tires. The plies make up the structure of a tire and they are layers of rayon, nylon, polyester or steel cords beneath the tread and inside the rubber sidewalls. When you hear of a two or four ply tire, it only means the number of these plies (no matter what the material) beneath the tread.

Bias Ply

If you look at this type of tire head-on and could see beneath the tread, you would see a layer of cords running diagonally down

Passenger Tire Conversion Chart

Bias Ply	Bias and Belted Bias Ply			Radial Ply					
1965 and LATER	60 SERIES	70 SERIES	78 SERIES	60 SERIES	70 SERIES	78 SERIES	60 SERIES Millimeter	70 SERIES Millimeter	80 SERIES Millimeter
600-13		A70-13	A78-13	AR60-13	AR70-13	AR78-13		185/70-13	165-13
650-13	B60-13		B78-13	BR60-13		BR78-13			173-13
	C60-13		C78-13			CR78-13			
700-13	D60-13	D70-13	D78-13		DR70-13	DR78-13			185-13
				ER60-13		ER78-13			
645-14			B78-14			BR78-14		185/70-14	155-14
695-14		C70-14	C78-14		CR70-14	CR78-14	215/60-14	200/70-14	165-14
735-14	D60-14	D70-14	D78-14		DR70-14	DR78-14	225/60-14	205/70-14	175-14
775-14	E60-14	E70-14	E78-14		ER70-14	ER78-14	235/60-14	215/70-14	185-14
825-14	F60-14	F70-14	F78-14	FR60-14	FR70-14	FR78-14	245/60-14	225/70-14	195-14
855-14	G60-14	G70-14	G78-14	GR60-14	GR70-14	GR78-14	255/60-14	235/70-14	205-14
885-14	H60-14	H70-14	H78-14		HR70-14	HR78-14	265/60-14	245/70-14	215-14
	J60-14	J70-14	J78-14	JR60-14	JR70-14	JR78-14	275/60-14		225-14
	L60-14	L70-14			LR70-14				
600-15			A78-15			AR78-15		185/70-15	165-15
						BR78-15			
685-15	C60-15	C70-15	C78-15		CR70-15	CR78-15		195/70-15	175-15
735-15		D70-15	D78-15		DR70-15	DR78-15		205/70-15	185-15
775-15	E60-15	E70-15	E78-15	ER60-15	ER70-15	ER78-15	215/60-15	215/70-15	195-15
825-15	F60-15	F70-15	F78-15	FR60-15	FR70-15	FR78-15	225/60-15	225/70-15	205-15
855-15	G60-15	G70-15	G78-15	GR60-15	GR70-15	GR78-15	235/60-15	235/70-15	215-15
885-15	H60-15	H70-15	H78-15	HR60-15	HR70-15	HR78-15	245/60-15	245/70-15	225-15
900-15	J60-15	J70-15	J78-15	JR60-15	JR70-15	JR78-15	255/60-15		
		K70-15			KR70-15				
915-15	L60-15	L70-15	L78-15	LR60-15	LR70-15	LR78-15	265/60-15		230-15

from left to right and on top of that layer would be another layer of cords running diagonally down from right to left. By crisscrossing the layers and cords, the strength of the tire is greatly increased.

Belted Bias Ply

This type of tire construction uses the same crisscrossing layers of cords, but between these layers and the actual tire tread there are more layers of finer cords running around the circumference, or "belting" the tire. Doing this minimizes tire squirming and keeps the tread flatter on the road.

Belted Radial Tires

Radial design tires also use layers or plies of cords but instead of diagonally crisscrossing each other, the layers run from side-to-side or across the tire. Then, beneath these layers at least two more layers run around the circumference of the tire, or "belt" it. The advantage here is that the tread is much firmer on the road and squirms less even though the sidewalls are more flexible. Because the tread is firm and the sidewalls flexible, the radial tire often looks soft or slightly flat even with the correct air pressure. Don't be alarmed, this is the way they are supposed to look.

Most professionals and consumers will agree that the superior tire is steel belted and radial design. The radial design is stronger, safer and lasts longer and the steel belts make it extremely safe and resistant to early wear. Although steel belted radials are quite a bit more expensive than other types, they can prove to be more economical in the long run. Most are guaranteed to last for 40,000 miles or about twice as long as polyester belted tires; they are almost impervious to blowouts and punctures and because of their tread design they eliminate the need for snow tires in all but severe winter areas.

Now that you know the differences among tires, don't make the mistake of mixing different designs and sizes on the same car. All four tires on any car should be the same size and radials should *never* be mixed with other tire types.

Electrical Checks You Can Make

The easiest and probably most important check you can make are the battery cables. I hope you remember where they are (attached to the battery terminals or posts)? One cable (Positive) goes to the starter motor at the bottom rear of the engine, and the other cable (Negative) is grounded by being bolted to the car's frame or to the engine.

Do you see a white, fluffy, powdery substance where the cables attach to the battery? If so, this is acid or corrosion and it is dangerous so don't get it near your eyes. If it should come in contact with your skin, wash it off right away. It will also eat holes in your clothes so when you clean the battery terminals, wear old gloves and old clothes or an apron.

The best way to clean off this corrosion is with a pail of water, a brush and some baking soda which neutralizes the acid. Make sure the battery caps are on tight, then dump water on the battery and scrub it, case and terminals, with the brush and the baking soda. Rinse it well but if you use a hose, cover the rest of the engine with a plastic sheet or a tarp for if you wet the engine, it probably won't start. Whenever you wash off this acid in the driveway or garage, also wash down the floor or it will turn brown.

Believe it or not, loose or corroded cables are one of the most common causes of breakdown on the road. To make the best possible contact, cables should actually be removed from the battery and the battery terminals—as well as the insides of the cable ends—should be thoroughly cleaned with sandpaper or steel wool. If you do this yourself, be sure to remove the positive cable *first* and attach it *last*. To remove the cables, simply loosen the bolt across the end which keeps the cable end clamped onto the battery post.

I'm sure you don't need to be told that if you see smoke coming from the wiring, immediately shut the car off. Besides risking further damage by continuing to drive, a spark could easily ignite some gasoline and cause a fire or explosion.

Lights

There is certainly no reason why you can't check to see that all the lights work, is there? On a turn you may think your signals are working but if they are not, this is a good way to get klunked in the rear end. Brake lights are also extremely important and should be checked often. I hear of many rear-end accidents caused by the brake lights not working. By making a quick check every once in a while, you can avoid that possibility.

In the front check both headlights, both high beams, both parking lights and both turn signals.

In the rear check both taillights, both turn signals, both brake lights and the backup lights. For checking the backup lights and the brake lights, a helper will make the job much easier.

If anyone of these lights do not work and the rest of the system functions normally, there are four main possibilities (in order of probability): 1) the bulb/socket assembly has come out of the light housing; 2) the bulb has burned out; 3) the fuse has blown; 4) the connecting wire is bad.

If the bulb/socket assembly has been knocked out of the housing, put it back in and all lights and indicators should work again.

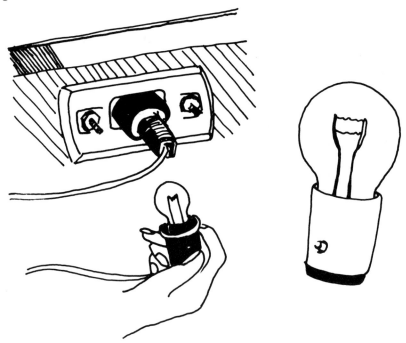

Removing and replacing plug-in taillight bulbs.

It is usually easiest to find out whether the bulb has burned out and this can be done by removing and testing it. Automotive light bulbs are pretty standard items (with the exception of headlights) in that they look the same and are removed and installed in their sockets in the same way. The difference from car to car will be gaining access to the bulb. Some taillights, for example, are reached by removing the outer, red plastic lens; others can be removed from the back of the taillight assembly somewhere in the trunk.

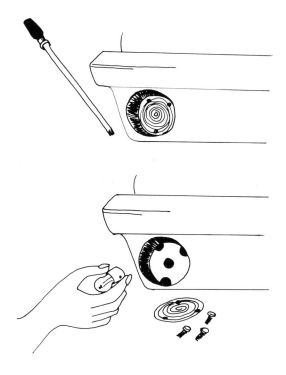

Removing the outer lens.

When the light in question is any *but* the headlight, check first to see whether the lens cover can be unscrewed or pried off from the outside or, if it cannot, whether the socket and bulb pulls out from the back of the light assembly. Once you reach the bulb, push it in, turn it to one side and pull it out. This procedure applies to any outside lights, except the headlights, and to the interior dome light.

To test the bulb, first examine it carefully. If the filaments inside are broken, replace it. Next, examine the area where the bulb makes contact with the socket; if corrosion is present, this could be the cause of the light not working. This would be especially possible if the light works intermittently or blinks. To repair a corroded connection, polish the area with fine sandpaper or fine steel wool then blow the dust away. If neither of these visible indicators are present, either put that bulb into the socket of the other light (if you know that one works) or try a new replacement bulb. If the light still does not work, move on to the second possibility: fuses.

Fuses

Fuses are little cartridge-like items that are inserted into an electrical system somewhere between the power source and the fixture. Their purpose is to absorb an electrical overload in the line and blow out or break the circuit rather than letting the overload continue and burn out the wire and bulb on the other end. Fuses and circuit breakers serve the same purpose and are similar in function, if not appearance, to the fuses and circuit breakers in your cellar.

The fuse box in most cars is located underneath the dashboard, usually on the driver's side, and it will contain a row or rows of several fuses. Each fuse is small, cylindrical and glass with metal caps on each end. The fuse clamps into its holder at these metal ends and they are what allow the circuit to be completed through the fuse. The fuse can be removed by popping it straight out of the end clamps. The circuit that the fuse controls will usually be identified right next to it on the fuse box, i.e. "heater/defroster" or "headlights" or "radio." So locating the proper fuse should be no problem. After you remove it, look into the glass part and you will see a small metal strip; if that metal strip is burned and/or broken, replace it.

Replacement fuses and light bulbs can be purchased at your gas station and they can be identified by numbers printed right on them.

If you are sure the bulb is good and the fuse is good, the problem gets a little more complicated but there are a few more things you can check before turning the car over to a garage. If, for example, your left rear taillight is not working, you will be warned by the left turn signal indicator on the dashboard lighting but not flashing. Of course, this could also indicate the the left *front* parking light/turn signal is not functioning because of a bad bulb but at least you have isolated the problem to one of two bulbs, and a visual check can show whether it is in the front or rear. If the problem were a blown fuse, a faulty flasher mechanism, or a bad connecting wire, the dashboard turn signal indicator would not light at all.

Dashboard Lights

The dashboard bulbs, whether they be instrument lights or courtesy lights which go on when the door is opened, can be removed and replaced in the same manner as the other bulbs mentioned earlier. However, dashboard bulbs are very small and your biggest problem when trying to replace them will be gaining access to them in the limited space behind the dashboard. If, for example, a particular instrument light is not working and the fuse is in good shape, you will first have to locate the back of that instrument underneath the dashboard. With the maze of wires and gadgets under there this search may take you a few minutes. The time-tested method is to lie on your back with your legs dangling out the driver's door (having put the front seat all the way back) and examine the area with a flashlight. If the underdash area is unusually complicated or inaccessible, feeling around with your hand may be the only solution. You will be looking for a wire and socket entering the back of the dashboard and, like the outside lights, it can be pulled out with the bulb still in it. The bad bulb can then be used to secure a replacement and you will probably have to "feel" it back into place.

Like any other do-it-yourself operation I discuss in this book, don't be scared to give it a try. At worst you will have to invest a little of your time but you won't hurt anything and even if the job is too difficult for you, you will have gotten a better feel for what a car is all about and how it works.

Four-Way Flashers

The four-way flasher system or emergency blinkers is really just a switch that makes both turn signals blink at once. Their use as a safety device is important enough that you should fix them right away should they not be functioning for some reason. The first thing to check is whether the turn signals work. If they also do not work, the problem will be in one of the bulbs or fuses. If they do work and the flashers do not, check the separate flasher fuse or the wiring to and from the flasher switch which will be either on the steering column or on the dashboard.

Headlights

When headlights go bad, they burn right out rather than weakening first. If one of the headlights is not working, chances are good that the bulb has burned out although the possibility still exists that a fuse has blown. With a nonfunctioning headlight it is easier to check the fuse before checking the bulb. Headlight fuses will be plainly marked on the fuse box and, like any other fuse, examine the metal filament inside the glass part of the fuse. If the fuse looks good to you, assume that the bulb has burned out.

To remove a headlight you must first remove the outside ring which protects the rim of the headlight. Once that has been removed (usually held on by two screws), you will see several screws which hold the headlamp itself in place. Unscrew these and pull the lamp out a few inches. The inside end of the lamp will be plugged into a receptacle much like a plug at home. Pull the plug out and then plug the new one in and screw it back into place like the one you removed. But keep in mind that when you unscrewed the old headlamp, you upset the exact aim of the headlights toward the road. You cannot reestablish this yourself as headlights must be aimed by a pretty sophisticated machine. Before replacing the outer ring, take the car to your gas station to have the headlights aimed.

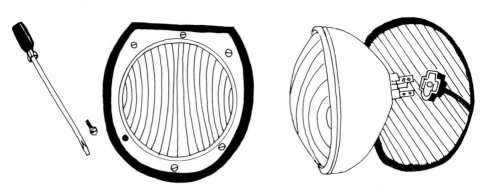

Removing and replacing headlight bulbs.

Windshield Wipers

The importance of a clean windshield is too obvious to restate but if people's acceptance of this importance can be judged by how they maintain their car's washers and wipers, then I have to conclude that most people like to take big chances.

The windshield wiper system consists of a small electric motor under the dashboard or under the hood. A belt attached to this motor drives both wiper arms back and forth across the windshield. A rubber blade is attached to each wiper arm and as the arm goes from side to side, the blade flops over slightly so that on the way back across the windshield it scrapes off the water drops.

A windshield wiper arm and slide-out rubber blade.

With a slight drizzle falling on a dirty windshield, you can see how the result will be mud. This is why the washer system was added and it merely pumps water or cleaning solution out of a small bottle and against the windshield.

There are two checks required to maintain this system. Regularly check and maintain the level in the washer bottle, and check the condition of the wiper blades frequently. The blades are only made of rubber, which they must be to do their job correctly, and rubber wears out after extended use. Replacement blades only cost a few dollars and good ones could prevent an accident while worn ones could cause an accident by blurring your vision in the rain.

Exterior Problems

Seeing is believing, and there are a lot of things you can see and fix yourself or at least see and *have* fixed, so keep your eyes peeled for visible defects on the outside of the car.

One very common automobile ailment, which humans also get, is called cancer. The first sign of cancer usually occurs around the chrome strips and headlights or in the rocker panels (the strip of body below the door). Salt water that does not drain off or not washing your car after driving through road salt in the winter can cause a small rust spot on the inside of the body. This will then eat away to a larger hole which is why it is called cancer. Once it starts, the cure is to get the car to a reliable body shop and have it refinished. You can prevent it or at least retard it by washing and waxing at regular intervals.

Loose Chrome or Exterior Parts

In many states loose chrome, rusted-out areas and unrepaired body damage can be the cause of a car failing the state inspection. This is because such protrusions and sharp edges are extremely dangerous, especially when on a moving object such as a car. Take a good look at your car to see whether such things exist and either have them repaired by a body shop or, if minor, try to correct them yourself. A by-product of your attention will be a car that looks better, stays newer longer and maintains its resale value longer.

Water Leaks

If your washing machine leaked, wouldn't you fix it? Sure you would. Well do the same for your car.

Look under the hood at all the water hoses and the areas where they connect to each other or to the radiator or engine. If there is a leak, it will usually be around a connection near the hose clamp (that ring around the end of the hose which has a screw to tighten it).

Also check the radiator from the outside and underneath but don't confuse leaks with the overflow tube of the radiator. Another word of caution: *Never* remove the radiator cap when the engine is warm. As I mentioned before, this is disaster. Cooling systems in today's cars are under such high pressure (up to 18 pounds) that it is like taking the lid off a pressure cooker while it is on the stove.

Check behind the water pump for signs of water or rust running down the side. This indicates an erratic leak. It may leak either while you are driving along or else just sitting but it nevertheless indicates a leak.

While checking for leaks you can also take a look at the heater inside the car. The most obvious sign of a leak here is water on the floor of the car. Another sign of a heater leak is if steam rises and clouds the windshield when you turn the defroster on. Most car heaters are very hard to remove, take apart, repair and reinstall. Heater repair is no job for an amateur so make sure it is the heater that is defective before running to an expensive professional.

Valve Cover Leaks

Perhaps you have noticed an oily, hot smell in your car especially when the heater is on, or there may be smoke coming from under the hood. If you lift the hood chances are good that you will see oil leaking from under the valve cover (the cover on top of the cylinder head) down onto the very hot exhaust manifold and smoking. To correct this, the valve cover must be removed and a new gasket installed between the cover and the cylinder head. This job is not extremely complex but it should be reserved for the advanced do-it-yourselfer.

Maintenance Interval Chart

ENGINE	*FREQUENCY (MONTHS/MILES)*
Change engine oil and filter	3/3,000
Check engine oil level	Every fuel stop
Adjust carburetor: idle speed and mixture	Every tune-up/10-12,000
Replace carburetor air cleaner cartridge	12/12,000
Clean oil filler cap	Every tune-up/10-12,000
Check engine accessory drive belts	6/6,000
Replace PCV valve	24/24,000
Check ignition timing	Every tune-up/10-12,000
Check spark plugs and points	Every tune-up/10-12,000
Replace fuel filter	24/24,000
Replace radiator coolant	24/24,000
Check coolant level	6/6,000
Clean and inspect distributor cap and rotor	Every tune-up/10-12,000

Maintenance Interval Chart—*continued*

Inspect radiator hoses for deterioration, leaks and loose hose clamps	12/12,000
Check power steering fluid level	6/6,000
Check brake master cylinder fluid level	6/6,000
Check battery fluid level	3/3,000
Inspect fuel lines, pump and filter for leaks	12/12,000
Inspect ignition wiring	12/12,000
Adjust valves (mechanical type)	12/12,000
Check transmission fluid level (automatic or standard)	3/3,000
CHASSIS	
Lubricate:	
front ball joints and universal joints	6/6,000
transmission linkage	24/24,000
Check:	
brake lines and linings	12/12,000
tire pressure	3/3,000
front wheel alignment	6/6,000
real axle fluid	6/6,000
air-conditioning system	Beginning of every season or every 12 months
Inspect, clean and repack wheel bearings	24/24,000
Rotate tires	12/12,000
BODY	
Lubricate:	
Door striker pins	24/24,000
Door hinge pivots	24/24,000
Door lock cylinders	6/6,000
Hood and trunk hinges	24/24,000
Hood latch and safety latch	24/24,000
Trunk latch	24/24,000
Trunk lock cylinder	6/6,000
Seat tracks	24/24,000
Check headlight aim	12/12,000
Clean body and door drain holes	12/12,000
Replace wiper blades	24/24,000

Chapter 6

If It Won't Start

Under The Hood

Back to that workhorse under the hood: the engine with all its gadgets and components. If it is not running smoothly as it normally should, it will usually speak out and tell you about it. In fact, this goes for almost the whole car: if something is wrong, you will be the first to hear. So don't ignore any unusual noises you may notice because this is the way the car communicates problems.

Keep in mind that there are three factors necessary for the engine to start and run. They are electricity, fuel and mechanical condition. If any one of these factors is not present or working properly, the car will probably not start and, if it does, it definitely won't run properly. In fact, when you have a car tuned you are restoring the proper relationship between the electrical, fuel and mechanical systems of the engine.

If the correct amount of electrical charge is not combined with the proper amount of fuel at the exact time, and if the mechanical parts are not working smoothly and properly, trouble is imminent. As you can imagine, getting all these systems to operate in the right way and at the right time is no easy task. The basic job of making it all work in the first place was done originally when the car was built. Keeping it that way, restoring it to original efficiency or knowing when it has worn out of whack is up to you or your mechanic.

Starting

The first noise that you hear upon turning the key is the starter motor turning over. It should have a solid, smooth sound and should *not* be raspy, groaning or hesitant. If any of these noises occur, the starter needs attention and may need parts replaced such as the armature shaft bushings, brushes or solenoid switch.

If the only noise you hear when you turn the key on is a click, the solenoid switch is not working properly. The solenoid switch is mounted on the starter motor and it closes the circuit between the battery and the starter motor. If this switch only clicks, it means that there is enough juice to operate the switch but not enough to turn the starter motor. Often this indicates either a bad connection to the battery or a badly discharged battery which just can't put out enough of a charge to turn the starter.

If, when you turn the key, the starter gives out a loud whining or spinning noise, there are two possibilities:

1. The starter drive is slipping;
2. The battery is very low. To find out which it is, first test the battery to see whether it is fully charged. If it is, check the cables for looseness or corrosion. One way to tell whether the cables are at fault is to turn the lights on and try to start the car. If the cables are loose, you may hear a crackling noise caused by the terminals not making good contact on the battery posts.

If the battery is fully charged and the terminals are clean and tight, check the connector at the solenoid on top of the starter. Many times I have found that the nut which holds the cable to the solenoid was loose and causing trouble.

If the starter still won't turn over, it's time for a visit to the garage where chances are good that the whole starter will have to be removed and either rebuilt or replaced.

Remember that only a car with a standard transmission can be jump started. To do this, put the car in Second gear and keep the clutch pedal *in*. Turn the key on and get someone to push the car. When you pick up a fair speed, release the clutch and the engine will fire. Give it some gas to keep it going and you're on your way. You *cannot* do this with an automatic transmission and you can severely damage that expensive component by trying to jump start it.

Fuel

If the starter is turning the engine over but the car will not start, it is possible that fuel is not getting all the way from the gas tank into the cylinder to be ignited. Elementary as it may sound, make sure there is gas in the tank. A metal tube connects the tank to the fuel pump on the engine so if there is still gas in the tank, you can assume that the gas line is not broken.

Most fuel problems are located in the carburetor, a device which must be properly tuned to do its job effectively. To see if it is at least letting fuel through, remove the air cleaner from its top. Then pull the linkage on its side forward (which is the same as pumping the gas pedal) and look down into the carburetor to see whether fuel is being sprayed downward into the holes in the bottom of the carburetor. If gas is getting through, the problem is *probably* not in the fuel system but in the electrical system. If gas is not getting through, you will have to check the fuel pump to see whether gas is even getting to the carburetor.

But before doing that, a less serious problem could be vapor lock. On a hot day vapor lock in the fuel line can block the flow of fuel to the carburetor. Allow the engine to cool and thereby disperse the bubbles which are blocking the fuel line. If you are in a hurry, pouring cold water over the fuel line will help.

The fuel pump is a mechanical device which is run by the engine so if the engine can be turned by the starter, it will operate the fuel pump. To make sure that the fuel pump is delivering gas to the carburetor, find the pipe that connects the pump to the carburetor and unscrew it at the carburetor. Put a can or a rag at the end of this pipe and turn the starter over. If the pump is functioning, it will pump gas out of the pipe and into the can or rag. Check to see whether there is any kind of filter on the gas line between the pump and carburetor. If there is, it could be clogged and by removing it and turning the starter over, you can discover if the blockage is there.

Electricity

Of course you will remember that the source of electricity in a car is the battery and if it is dead, the starter will not turn over. But if the battery is good and the starter turns over, there can still be electrical problems which will prevent the car from starting. Chapter Five describes how an engine works and, to summarize the electrical system, current originates in the battery, goes through the ignition key to the starter, continues on to the coil, then to the distributor, and finally to the spark plugs. Before we even count individual parts and wires, there are six steps that electrical current must pass through on its trip. The point is don't be fooled into thinking that a problem cannot be electrical just because the starter turns over and the battery has a good charge.

Having found out that the fuel system is functioning properly or at least delivering gas to the carburetor, you can now begin to eliminate possible electrical problems. Assuming the worst, that you are stuck by the side of the road with no testing equipment and only basic tools, the following troubleshooting procedures are elementary but reliable.

If the battery has enough power to turn the starter motor strongly, you can assume that the electrical problem lies between the starter and the inside tip of the spark plug. From there on you will be eliminating possible problem locations until you find the malfunction.

First, make sure that all of the cables are firmly attached to the distributor, then inspect each of those cables making sure that they are not broken and that the other ends are firmly attached to the spark plugs and to the coil. Pull one of the cables off of a spark plug and hold it near the exhaust manifold. Turn the starter over and a healthy spark should jump from the cable end to the manifold. If this does happen, replace that cable and do the same thing to a few more cables. If there is a spark, it means that the current has made it all the way through the electrical system but it cannot make the spark plugs fire. Either the plug is defective in some way or, more likely, the firing end is too dirty to fire properly or at all. If this is the case, unscrew the spark plug with a socket or plug wrench and, with your nail file, clean off the little "L" shaped tip of the plug. This tip is called the electrode. Very carefully bend the electrode back toward the plug body—just a hair will do. Replace the plug, reattach the cable and do the same for the other plugs. Now start the car.

If the spark plug test produces no spark, you can assume that the trouble lies between the starter and the end of the cables. If a visual inspection of the spark plug cables and the terminals at each end of them, the distributor cap, the cable from the distributor cap to the coil, the wire from the coil to the ignition switch, and the ignition switch itself shows no obvious problems such as breaks, cracks, disconnections, burns or bad fits—then the malfunction is probably inside one of the electrical components.

Leaving the cables *attached,* unclamp or unscrew the distributor cap and look inside it for burns or faulty connections. Then look down inside the distributor for burn marks on the rotor, burned and pitted points or an improper point gap. You won't be able to see too large or small a gap but if that is the problem, the points themselves should show the ill effects.

Mechanical

If your car will not start and has been reasonably well maintained, chances are pretty good that the problem is either in the electrical or fuel system. The third possibility, mechanical mal-functions, will usually only occur on older or abused automobiles and this means parts that are either broken or worn beyond the point where they can do their job. Worn piston rings, bent connecting rods, broken timing chain, worn, bent or broken valves, a worn-out oil pump and worn bearings are some of these mechanical failures.

Troubleshooting and repairing them is strictly an expensive professional job, but preventing them is the whole point of preventive maintenance. If one of these mechanical problems or failures should occur, it will most likely be preceded by very harsh and unusual noises and/or billows of smoke.

Piston rings, connecting rods, timing chains and gears, valves and bearings should last at least 70,000 miles on a car that is maintained well. Regular changing of the oil and oil filter can alone contribute to these parts lasting well over 100,000 miles. The cost of not maintaining these parts is high: rebuilding the engine or overhauling the cylinder heads will cost hundreds of dollars, all of which can be cheaply avoided by you.

Overheating

If you see on the temperature gauge that the engine is over-heating, there is some problem in the cooling or exhaust system. If the car overheats to the point where it boils over, there is a major problem which must be attended to right away.

In most cases, flushing out the radiator and cooling system passages, checking the thermostat and then adding the proper amount of antifreeze will solve slight overheating problems. If the overheating is caused by the system losing coolant, check the radiator and hoses for leaks; such leaks will leave a stain which aids in pinpointing their location.

However, I have had some strange experiences with customers bringing in overheating cars. One person came to me with both overheating and a loss of power. He said that one garage had checked the timing, thermostat and cooling system and found all to be in good shape. I checked it and found that the exhaust system was partially clogged. A closed heat riser had caused this; the exhaust could not escape and the engine got too hot.

I had another problem with similar symptoms where a garage had concluded that the car had a slipping transmission which they fixed. This other garage also said the radiator was too small and replaced it; they also checked the timing and removed the thermostat. When it came to me, I checked it on a lift and found that when accelerating suddenly there was practically no exhaust. I cut the muffler in half and found that one of its baffles had come loose so that it was shutting off the exhaust pipe during acceleration. At idle the baffle fell back into place and everything seemed normal. This is a case in a million but it illustrates the necessity of methodical and accurate diagnosis and treatment. It also shows how long it may take to locate a knotty problem. Most importantly it shows that a careful and accurate description of the problem by you the customer will give the mechanic more to go on and require less time for exploration. If your car has a difficulty, write down anything that does not seem normal to you, whether or not you think it is related to the basic problem.

How To Use Jumper Cables

Jumper cables are used to give a dead battery a charge from a good battery in another car. They are simply two long cables with big clips on each end. One cable connects the positive terminals of each battery and the other cable connects the two negative terminals. If you are smart, you will buy a set and keep them in your car.

However, jumper cables can be dangerous if you don't know how to use them. Follow these instructions and you will have no problem. Keep in mind that with anything electric, if you touch the positive and negative terminals at the same time, your body is completing the circuit.

1. Find the positive and negative terminals on your battery and on the battery you are jumping from. Stamped near the terminals will be the "+" and "−" signs. If you cannot find such marks, follow both cables to their other ends. The negative cable will just be attached by a bolt to the engine or frame. The positive cable will attach to the starter and usually will be longer than the negative cable.

2. Always attach a positive terminal to a positive terminal with one cable, and always attach a negative terminal to a negative terminal with the other cable.

If you reverse this connection rule, you can blow up the battery, hurt yourself and damage the alternator and regulator. One spark is all that is necessary because a lot of gas is emitted from the battery.

3. When the cables are attached correctly and the car you are jumping *from* is running, try to start the dead car.

What you are actually doing is using the other car's battery to start your car; you are not really recharging your battery.

4. As soon as your dead car starts and you can keep it going, disconnect the cables, removing them from the dead car first.

Because getting a jump only started your car but did not recharge the battery, you will either have to drive your car until the alternator recharges the battery or you will have to have the battery recharged on a slow charging machine (found at most gas stations).

Front End Problems

Few motorists think about the effects that high mileage and rough road conditions have on their car. Worn tires and a loose front end will reduce control on ice- and snow-covered roads and will contribute to skidding and loss of control.

The condition of tires and major front end components like shocks, springs, tie-rods and ball joints which take quite a beating should be checked before aligning the front end or balancing the wheels. Loose ball joints will prevent the front end from being aligned correctly and bad shocks will prevent the front end from holding an alignment for very long. So when you take your car in for an alignment, have other related components checked also. The best way to prevent early front end wear is a regular chassis lubrication.

Some symptoms of front end wear or misalignment are: high speed shimmy, vibration noises, tires which wear unevenly, hard steering, pulling to one side and shimmying when you hit a bump. Some of these conditions may also indicate wheels which need

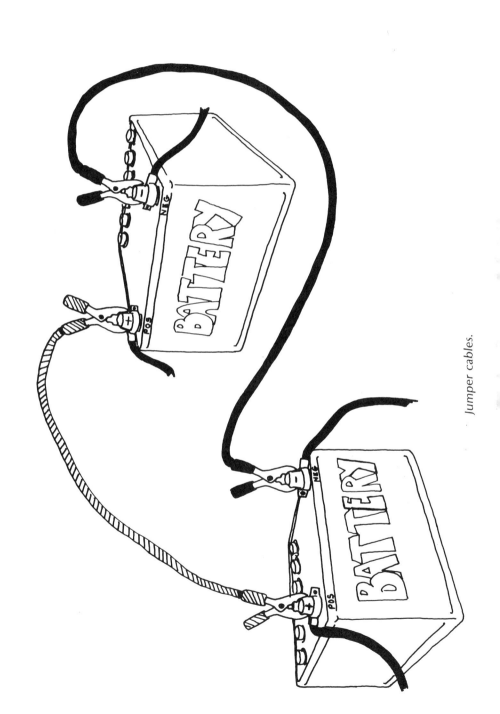

Jumper cables.

balancing or adjustment of the brakes; but whatever the cause, such conditions are unsafe, money wasting and contributors to poor gas mileage.

Other Noises

Valve Tap
Sometimes when a car is first started a loud tap, tap, tap noise can be heard from under the hood, This is commonly called valve tap and on cold mornings is not too unusual. During the night the oil in the engine drains back down into the oil pan and low temperatures make it thick. When you first start the car the oil isn't hot enough (and therefore thinner) to get all the way up into the top of the engine where the valves are. Therefore they tap or knock because there is not enough oil to smooth the way. After the car warms up, this tapping noise should stop.

If the tapping does not stop when the car warms, there could be a more serious problem. If the oil and filter has not been changed often enough, it may be so thick and sludgy that it cannot go where it is supposed to and the valves, because they are not being lubricated, will tap. Another possibility is that the valves themselves are worn out but this should not be the case if the oil is changed frequently unless the car has extremely high mileage on the odometer. A remote possibility for the source of valve tap is low oil pressure caused by a gasket leak, a worn oil pump, restricted oil passages or oil that is too thick. In any case, persistent valve tapping should be checked because further, more expensive trouble can result. Often a couple of oil changes or a cleansing additive will provide a cheap cure.

Exhaust
The most obvious exhaust noise is a bad muffler which is characterized by a roar as you accelerate. But such a roar doesn't necessarily have to be caused by a bad muffler. The pipes leading from the engine to the muffler may be rusted out or they may have come apart from vibration or scraping the road after a big bump. Look for the source of loud noises yourself to avoid being sold a whole new exhaust system when you may not really need one.

If, as you speed up, you hear a choppy, clattering noise from the engine area, the problem may be where the exhaust pipe meets the exhaust manifold. If things quiet down when the engine warms up, the gasket between these two pipes may have worn out. As the pipes heat up and expand, they tighten together and the noise diminishes.

Belts

A common but very irritating noise which usually occurs when the car is cold is fan belt squeal. This is caused by the drive belts slipping on their pulleys and it is a shrill squeal. Tightening the belts will probably cure it but it also may be an indication that the belts need to be replaced.

Spark Knock or "Ping"

If, when you accelerate hard, you can hear a ping, click or rattling noise, this is what is known as spark knock. There are several possible causes of spark knock most of which should be eliminated by a good tune-up. If the ignition timing is improperly set or the spark plugs are fouled or not gapped properly, spark knock can occur. One of the most common causes of spark knock, however, is using low octane gas in a car which requires a higher grade. Read your owner's manual for the recommended gas quality for your particular car and engine.

Dieseling

A sound that will scare you to death but which isn't too serious is dieseling. This happens when you shut off the engine and it keeps running. It will chug, jump, smoke and cough and, if you turn the key back on, the engine will just keep running. The only way to stop the engine from running is to put the transmission in drive and then shut the car off. The cause of dieseling is a combination of conditions: the car is idling too fast, the engine is too hot, the spark plugs are fouled and the carburetor is slightly out of adjustment. The cure for dieseling is a good tune-up which will eliminate these conditions.

Power Steering Squeal

Power steering is a real boon to all drivers and, of course, it makes parking so much easier. But, as I described in Chapter Four, it is driven by a pump and belts and this means components that can wear out and require maintenance. A slight hissing noise when you turn the wheel hard is normal but when that hiss becomes a squawk or whine, it is no longer normal. First check the fluid level in the pump; then check the power steering drive belt and the tire pressure.

Other Curious Sounds

If an unusual noise occurs only when the car moves, chances are good that it is in the running gear, suspension or transmission and not in the engine. Transmission noises will usually be accompanied by a roughness or hesitation in shifting or an inability to engage gears properly.

A persistent low rumble or droning noise can usually be narrowed to the wheel bearings or rear axle bearings which come from the factory packed in grease and should be checked once a year.

A clunking noise when you first start out when you accelerate rapidly and when you shift gears probably indicates that the universal joints are worn out. What, you may ask, are universal joints? Remember the driveshaft which connects the transmission to the differential in the rear axle? Well if this were a completely rigid connection, going over a bump or taking a hard corner could cause the driveshaft to snap. To make the drive train somewhat flexible, two universal joints are added to the system, one where the transmission connects to the driveshaft and another one where the driveshaft connects to the differential. A universal joint is like your wrist joint: it can make a 180° rotation, not just up and down but also side to side.

Squeaking Brakes

If, when you apply the brakes and come to a stop, you hear a loud screeching, scraping noise, there are two main possibilities:

1. The brake linings have worn so far down that the rivets which hold them on are scraping against the brake drum; or

2. The brake linings have gotten brake fluid on their surfaces from a leak in the wheel cylinder or brake line. Have this checked right away because a leak can cause brake failure and worn linings can ruin the drums also and cause a large extra expense.

Emergency Tricks

Frozen Door Lock

Did you ever come out on a wet, cold, sleety morning to find that moisture has frozen in the car door locks? You can insert the key but the lock won't turn. Rather than shouting or kicking the car door, get a pack of matches or a cigarette lighter and heat up the end of the door key. Then insert it into the lock and the heat will melt the ice and free the lock.

Can't Find the Trunk Key

If you have lost the trunk key and you don't want to damage the car by prying it open, there is a longer but better way to get into the trunk. Remove the back seat bottom by pulling forward and lifting up. The seat back must then be removed and they are usually held on by clips or bolts at the bottom. Undo the bolts or clips and lift it up and out. You will then be able to see through to the trunk but there will be supports in the way so you won't be able to squeeze through. However, by using your flashlight and a long probe of some sort, you can reach through and release the trunk latch to open the trunk.

Can't Find the Ignition Key

If you have lost your keys altogether, this isn't too much of a problem on older cars that are not equipped with a lock switch on the steering column.

If you can get a mechanic to help you, he can "hot wire" the ignition like the best of car thieves.

Of course, the best solution to this situation is to be prepared beforehand. Write down the numbers from your keys and keep them in your wallet. If you lose them, a car dealership will probably be able to make you a new set with the numbers. Needless to say, the smartest trick would be to keep a spare set in your pocketbook and another at home.

Chapter 7

Fix It Yourself

Oil Change

If you have read through to this point, you cannot have missed the many times I have referred to the extreme importance of regularly changing the oil and oil filter. Doing this yourself is not too difficult and it will definitely save you some money—maybe 50%. You will need the following things to change the oil yourself:

1. *Oil.* It is usually cheaper to buy it by the case at an automotive or discount store. Be sure to read the oil grade on the top of the can or on the outside of the case.

2. *Spout.* This gadget punctures the top of the oil can and stays attached to it so you can pour the oil without spilling on the engine.

3. *Oil Filter.* Also available at automotive and discount stores, you will often pay less if you buy several. Be sure it is the correct one for your car and engine.

4. *Drain Pan.* A metal pan which is low enough to fit under the engine and which holds a little more than the capacity of your car's oil system will do the trick. You may have one around the

house or, if not, try the same automotive or discount store where you purchase the oil and filter.

5. *Oil Filter Wrench.*

How To Do It

The best time to change the oil is after you have driven the car enough for it to have reached its regular operating temperature. At this time the oil in the engine will be hotter and thinner and will therefore have picked up all the loose deposits it possibly can.

While the engine is still hot, jack up the front of the car slightly or drive it up on a curb or ramp enough to get the pan beneath the engine and for you to be able to reach under. If your car is not too low to the ground, jacking may not be necessary.

As I mentioned earlier, the oil pan is on the very bottom of the engine and it has a drain plug on its bottom with a head fitted for a wrench. When you locate this plug, unscrew it slowly until it falls into the drain pan. Then let all the oil drain out; this should take about ten or fifteen minutes but be generous so that everything has time to come out.

While the engine is draining, find the oil filter. As I said earlier, this is about the size of a tin can and the top end of it screws onto the engine, usually at the left front. Sometimes this filter can be unscrewed by hand but if it can't, slip the oil filter wrench around it and unscrew it. As you do, oil will drip out so try to have the drain pan positioned so it can catch this oil also.

Throw away the old filter and screw the new one on with your hands only—do not use the oil filter wrench to tighten the new filter. After you have replaced the filter, carefully pull the drain pan from under the car and (ugh) find the drain plug. A magnet or some probing device would be handy here.

Replace the drain plug in the oil pan. Use the wrench but do not tighten it with all your might. Now unscrew the oil filler cap from the top of one of the cylinder heads. Using the spout, punch a can of oil, fit the spout down onto it and quickly place the end of the spout in the filler hole.

Your owner's manual will tell you how many quarts of oil the engine holds, with and without a new filter. Remember, the filter holds an extra quart of oil so if you replace it, you must add that extra quart to the system. Add the necessary number of quarts to

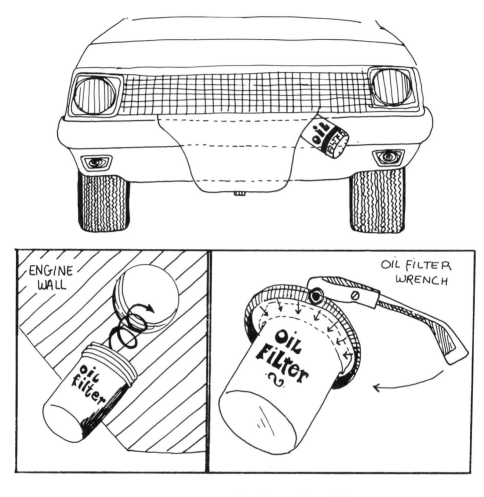

Changing the oil and replacing the oil filter.

fill the system and replace the oil filler cap. Check the level with the dipstick to make sure you have sufficient oil and the job will be finished.

The next question is what to do with five or six quarts of old oil? Some people pour it on their dirt driveway to keep the dust down. Some people use it as a preservative on fence posts and railroad ties. Other folks pour it into plastic jugs, cap them and put it in the trash. Whichever disposal method you use, try to first think of some practical way to reuse it or an ecological method of getting rid of it.

Lubrication

Many people who change their own oil also grease the car themselves. However, this job is a sloppier one and involves crawling underneath the car and working on your back so you may want to leave it to the garage that can do it on a lift. If, however, the do-it-yourself spirit really has a hold on you, here is what you will need:

1. *Grease Gun.* This is really a small hand pump to force the grease into the fittings and joints and force the old grease out.

2. *Grease.* Grease will normally come packed in a cartridge that fits into the grease gun so you won't have to handle it.

Hopefully, your car's owner's manual will show where the grease points are on the chassis. If not, either locate them in a factory shop manual (which you can buy at a dealership) or in a consumer book devoted to do-it-yourself maintenance of your particular car. Once you find the grease fittings (there will be anywhere from five to fifteen depending on the car), you just attach the nozzle on the end of the pump hose to the nipple on the grease fitting and pump the grease gun two or three times to do the job.

Tune-Up

If you think tuning the car yourself is too complicated or too much work, you are wrong. Aside from being easy when you get the feel, it will give you that "I did it myself" satisfaction and save you quite a bit of money in the process.

When you tune up an engine, you are replacing those parts that are most perishable or that take the most abuse during engine operation. In addition, a tune-up is when interdependent parts and systems are adjusted and synchronized so that the engine will run at maximum efficiency and smoothness and minimum strain and wear. The following list contains parts that should be replaced during a regular tune-up (every 10,000–12,000 miles) as well as those parts that should be replaced at other, less frequent intervals. Those items marked with an asterisk are less critical and their replacement schedule is included. Furthermore, the few necessary tools for you to perform a tune-up yourself are listed. All such tools are inexpensive, one-time purchases whose cost can be spread over all the tune-ups you may do on any car you may own.

1. *Spark Plugs.*   Buy four, six or eight depending on the number of cylinders in your car's engine. Be sure to buy a name brand—available at automotive supply and discount stores. The size and type for your particular car is designated by a code number found printed on the old plugs and in your owner's manual.

2. *Spark Plug Gapping Gauge.*   An inexpensive little gadget, this tool is a one-time purchase and it is used to measure and bend the electrode tip of the spark plug to the proper distance or "gap" from the body of the plug.

3. *Spark Plug Socket Wrench.*   This tool is used to unscrew the spark plug from the engine easily. It is a socket which fits down over the plug and it has a handle on the other end to turn it. These come in a variety of styles, some including ratchet handles, extensions and breaker bars. The more sophisticated (and more expensive) versions will only be necessary if your car has a particularly big engine, a cramped and complicated engine compartment or spark plugs which are very difficult to reach. If you are in doubt, ask the salesperson or a mechanic for a recommendation.

4. *Spark Plug Cables*.*   These are the heavy cables which connect the distributor to the spark plugs and to the coil. They usually come in packages already cut to the proper length and fitted with the necessary tips and rubber boots. The rate at which they deteriorate will vary so every other tune-up is probably the earliest point when they should be replaced. If you are putting new ones on your engine, be sure to replace them one by one so there is no chance of connecting the wrong plug to the wrong distributor tower and therefore changing the order in which the cylinders are fired.

5. *Distributor Cap*.*   This is the black plastic cap with the cables coming out of the top. It should be replaced during every other tune-up but a careful examination during every tune-up is the best indicator of when it should be replaced. An inexpensive item, this also can be obtained at auto supply and discount stores.

6. *Points, Rotor & Condenser.*   Although these are really three separate items, I've grouped them because they are all distributor internal components and because they should be

replaced together at every tune-up. Their combined cost is very low ($3–5) and they can make a huge difference in the efficiency and smoothness of any engine.

7. *Feeler Gauge.* This looks something like a jackknife and it has several blades of varying thickness to use when "gapping" the points or setting them to the proper opening after installation. This is another one-time purchase and not at all expensive.

8. *Dwell Meter.* This gadget provides a different and slightly more efficient method of adjusting the point gap. Although it too is a one-time purchase, it is not cheap. I would term it an optional tool—reserved for the more serious hobbyist.

9. *Timing Light.* This device is essential for setting the ignition timing of the engine—one of the final adjustments made during a tune-up. Prices for a timing light vary with the quality but there are two general types: those which draw power from the car's battery and those which can be plugged into a home outlet. The plug-in type produces a more intense light which is therefore easier to see, especially if you are working outside in daylight.

10. *PCV Valve*.* This valve is one part of the emission control system on your car. As I mentioned in Chapter Five, the positive crankcase ventilation system recirculates fumes from the engine into the carburetor and through the combustion and exhaust process. The PCV valve is attached to one end of this recirculation hose and it should last for at least 25,000 miles. If and when it finally needs to be replaced, the cost is low.

11. *Fuel Filter*.* Every other tune-up is a good time to replace this item. Fuel filters are also inexpensive and easy to install and they provide protection from dirt for the more sensitive inner carburetor components.

12. *Air Filter*.* This is the replaceable inside cartridge of the air cleaner. Under normal conditions it should last for at least 20,000 miles. But in dusty, dirty driving conditions it, the PCV valve and the oil and filter should be changed more often.

13. *Carburetor Solvent.* This comes in a spray can and in a variety of brands—just be sure that it is especially for carburetors. It is an intense cleaning solvent which will dislodge dirt particles in the carburetor passages.

When going to an automotive supply or discount store to purchase the required tools and replacement parts, be sure that you are armed with the following information:

A. The year, make and model of your car. For example, 1974 Pontiac Ventura II Sedan.

B. The engine type, size, carburetion and exhaust system. For example, *V-8* (8 cylinders), *350* cubic inches, *two-barrel* carburetor, *single exhaust* (are there one or two exhaust pipes?).

Being able to give the salesperson this precise information will ensure that you get those tune-up parts that are correct for your specific car.

The Tune-Up

Having gathered all the parts and tools you will need and having reserved a Saturday morning for the job, reread the "Ignition" section of Chapter Five and locate the various components on your own car. Then reread this section thoroughly to make sure you have no serious questions about how to proceed. To simplify the job it is described in numbered steps with any optional step designated by an asterisk.

1. *Changing The Spark Plugs.*   Remove the new spark plugs from their packages and, using the plug gapper, measure the gap. Look in your owner's manual for the correct gap and bend the electrode tip on the new plugs to this gap. You can do this by bending the electrode in the necessary direction with the hooked part of the plug gapping tool. But do so gently and recheck the gap each time.

2. *Number The Spark Plug Cables.*   Before you remove the cables from the plugs wrap a piece of masking tape around the cables. With a pen write the number on the tape—starting from the front. For example, the first plug on the right would be #1 and then 2, 3, 4 toward the rear and 5, 6, 7, 8 from front to rear on the left side. The actual numbers don't matter as much as correctly matching cable to plug.

3. *Remove The Spark Plug Cables.*   Before removing the plugs, clean around them with a rag so that no dirt will fall down into the cylinders when the plugs are removed. To pull the cable from the plug, grasp it by the boot and tug outward. Remove the cables one by one and replace them right after you replace each plug.

4. *Remove The Spark Plugs.*   Place the socket of the spark plug wrench all the way down over the plug. Then turn the wrench counterclockwise until the spark plug unscrews and comes out. A little muscle may be required to start the plug out.

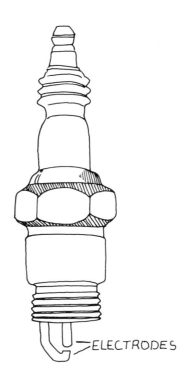

A spark plug.

5. *Install The New Spark Plug.*   Apply a few drops of oil to the threads (not the electrode) of the new plug and screw it into the engine with your hand. Then tighten it with the spark plug wrench without using too much pressure. Replace the cable to that plug and then proceed to the next plug using the same sequence of steps. When you have installed all new spark plugs, start the car and listen to it for a moment. If it runs very roughly and didn't before, you probably mixed up the cables so recheck them. Don't let the engine run long enough to get hot or the rest of the tune-up will be very difficult.

6. *Remove The Distributor Cap.*   This must be done without disturbing the spark plug cables coming out of the distributor cap. Distributors are held in place either by screws or by spring clips. If yours is held on by screws, undo them, pull the cap up and lay it to one side. If yours has clamps, snap them open, pull the cap up and lay it to one side. Look inside the cap for burn marks or pitting on the copper surfaces. If either is present, plan to replace the cap (at the end of the tune-up).

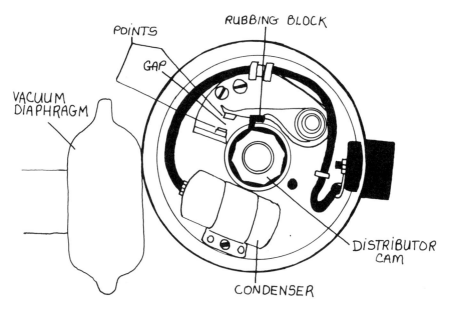

The inside of a distributor.

7. *Remove The Rotor.*   This is the plastic and copper item on the inside top of the distributor. Firmly pull it upward and off.

8. *Remove the Points and Condenser.*   Before doing this, take a good look at how it is put together, where things go and the relationship of pieces and wires. Using a screwdriver, remove the screw which holds the condenser to the floor of the distributor. *Be especially careful to keep this and any other screw from falling down into the distributor or a disaster could result.* The condenser is the shiny cylinder lying on its side with a short wire connecting it to a terminal. In order to remove the points this terminal will have to be disconnected but before doing so, study it carefully and

connect the new condenser to the terminal on the new points set. By doing this beforehand, you will only have to connect the non-removable distributor wire to the new terminal thereby diminishing your chances of making the connections incorrectly.

Having made these preparations, undo the two screws which hold the points set to the floor of the distributor. Again, be extremely careful to hang onto the screws so they won't fall down into the distributor. Loosen the terminal screw and remove the points set from the distributor.

9. *Install The New Points and Condenser.* Immediately put the new points set and condenser in place just exactly where the old ones were. Then carefully insert the condenser hold-down screw and tighten it while keeping the condenser in the correct position. Insert the two points set hold-down screws but don't tighten them completely—just enough to allow you to adjust positions. Clip the nonremovable distributor wire in place on the terminal and tighten the terminal screw fully.

At this point all the internal distributor components (except the rotor) have been replaced. All that remains is for you to adjust the points to the correct opening and tighten them down to the distributor floor—and this is the tricky part.

10. *Lubricate The Distributor Cam.* The distributor cam is that shaft sticking up in the middle of the distributor. It has several flat sides and each ridge formed by the meeting of these flat sides is called a lobe. There are as many lobes as the engine has cylinders— four, six or eight. In the points and condenser kit you will find a small capsule filled with grease. Open this capsule and, with your finger, smear this grease all the way around the distributor cam.

Now that you are more familiar with the internal parts of the distributor, a more detailed explanation of how it works will help you to adjust it properly. If you take a look at the coil you will see that it is connected to the distributor by a heavy cable and also by a thin wire. This thin wire runs up inside the distributor and is the nonremovable wire connected to the points terminal.

The coil is designed to send 12 volts of electricity (the amount produced by the 12-volt battery) through the thin wire into the distributor. This electrical charge comes through the terminal and then through to one side of the points set. If the points are closed, the circuit is completed and the charge passes on to the other side of the points set and is grounded—going nowhere.

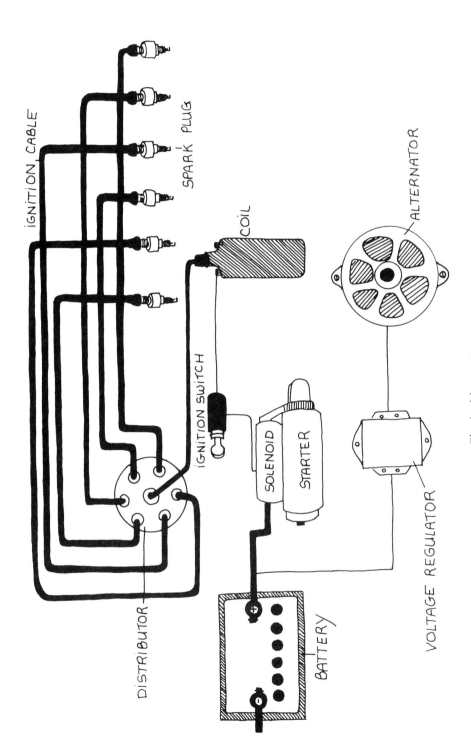

The ignition system.

If the points are open, however, and the current cannot pass through, this is a signal for the coil to perform its other function: to step up the 12-volt charge coming from the battery to 15,000-30,-000 volts. Of course, what decides whether the points are open or closed is the distributor cam: as the cam lobes come by the points their higher edge pushes the points open.

If the points are open and the coil therefore transforms 12 volts into 15,000, that charge is sent out from the top of the coil through the heavier wire that goes to the middle tower of the distributor cap. This charge runs through the center of the rotor and is sent to the outside end of the rotor. But the center shaft of the distributor (the extension of the distributor cam) is turning the rotor underneath the distributor cap. As the rotor turns, its outer end touches the inside end of the distributor towers and passes the high voltage current on to them one by one. That current then goes out through the distributor towers and continues through the cables to each spark plug.

As you can see, this is a complex process and timing it all to happen at just the right instances is very critical. When you gap the points and later set the ignition timing, you are synchronizing the whole system and causing all the parts to have the proper relationship to each other.

11. *Gap The Points.* Get out the feeler gauge with the blades and find that blade whose thickness corresponds to the point gap for your car. The point gap can be found in the owner's manual and is given in inches, such as 0.021 in.

The point gap which you are setting is the distance between the point contacts when they are open to the widest distance. As I explained, the points will be opened widest when one of the distributor cam lobes comes by and pushes them open. Therefore, in order to set this gap, one of the lobes (or high points) must be against the rubbing block of the points set. The distributor cam can be rotated to this position in two ways: you can try to turn the fan enough to turn the engine slightly and thereby rotate the distributor cam *or* you can have an assistant turn the ignition key a few times to accomplish the same thing. *If you choose the second method, make sure the car is in Neutral or Park, make sure that you are not touching anything while the ignition switch is on . . . and be careful of the fan.* Professional mechanics use a remote control ignition switch—a handy gadget which you may also buy at auto supply and discount stores.

When a distributor cam high point is against the point set rubbing block, insert the feeler gauge between the point contacts making sure that there is a snug fit. Still holding the gap with the feeler gauge blade, tighten the two point set hold-down screws down to the floor of the distributor. Remove the feeler gauge blade and then recheck the gap to make sure that it was not disturbed while tightening down the points set.

12. *Replace The Rotor.*   Install the new rotor on the distributor shaft. One side of the shaft is flat so the rotor can only go on in one way.

13. *Replace The Distributor Cap.*   The distributor cap will have a notch in its base to facilitate replacing it in the correct position. If you are installing a new cap, now is the time. Put the old cap back on the distributor with the cables still attached. Then place the new cap next to it in the same exact position. One by one transfer the cables from the old cap to the new one, being careful to transfer to' the proper towers. Transfer the coil cable last and then remove the old cap and install the new one in its place. Tighten down the screws or snap the clamps closed and that part of the tune-up (the major part) is finished.

14. *Checking The Points With A Dwell Meter.*   A dwell meter is a device which measures, in degrees, the length of time that the points are closed (the dwell). This is an indirect way of measuring how much the points are open—or their gap: the total number of degrees of distributor shaft rotation minus the dwell meter indication of how long the points are closed equals how long they are open.

To hook up the dwell meter, first disconnect that vacuum hose from the distributor and plug the hose end with a pencil or golf tee. Make sure the ignition switch is in the off position. The dwell meter will have two wires, one black (negative or ground) and one red (positive). Attach the black clip to a good ground such as a bolt on the engine block or to some part of the car's frame. Attach the red clip to that terminal on the coil which is connected by a wire to the distributor. Start the car and read the dwell meter. Make sure you are reading the correct scale for the number of cylinders in your car.

Remember that the dwell is an indirect measurement of the point gap so increasing the point gap will decrease the dwell and decreasing the point gap will increase the dwell. If your dwell meter registers a figure which is not in accordance with the dwell figure specified in your owner's manual, you will have to reset the point gap with the feeler gauge. If the dwell meter shows a figure above the specified one, you will have to increase the point gap (to decrease the dwell). If the dwell meter shows a figure below that specified, you will have to decrease the point gap (to increase the dwell). After you readjust the points, recheck the dwell and then disconnect the dwell meter.

15. *Install New Cables**.   If you plan to install new spark plug cables, now is the time to do so. Replacement cables usually come in sets already cut to the proper length and equipped with tips and boots. Remove the coil cable first and replace it last. Then remove the cables one by one, each time finding its replacement by size. When you have installed all the plug cables, then install the new coil cable and the job is done.

16. *Set The Ignition Timing.*   Remembering my discussion of how the distributor works, recall that the distributor shaft and cam is turned to open and close the points. The bottom part of the distributor shaft goes down inside the engine and it is turned by the crankshaft through gears. The timing of these gears must now be set correctly and this is where the timing light comes in.

On the bottom front of the engine you will see a large pulley which turns the fan belt. Somewhere on the circumference of the pulley a degree scale is stamped into the metal. Find that scale and wipe it off with a rag. A metal pointer is mounted on the engine so that the scale on the pulley passes underneath it. Wipe off the pointer also.

Look in your owner's manual for the correct ignition timing setting (in degrees). Then find this setting on the scale on the pulley (the scale will either be numbered or lined like a ruler in which case you must count the lines to the setting). Make a heavy mark right on the setting with a piece of chalk or a dab of Day-Glow paint. Make a similar mark on the pointer.

Instructions for hooking up the timing light will no doubt be included with the light but I will repeat them here so you will have a permanent reference. The timing light has two power supply leads to make the light flash: connect one to the positive battery terminal and the other lead to the negative battery terminal. The timing light will have a third wire to be connected to the Number One spark plug cable. Here, "Number One" is not necessarily the first plug in the engine but rather it is the first plug to be fired. So you will have to look in your owner's manual to find which plug is Number One. When you locate the Number One spark plug, follow its cable to the distributor and pull it out of the tower. Then plug the Number One spark plug cable (still connected to the plug) into the third timing light wire and insert the other end of the third timing light wire back into the Number One distributor tower.

You have now rigged up the timing light so that it will flash every time the Number One spark plug is fired. Make sure that the light and all the extra cables are not near the fan blades and then look for a small rubber hose connected to the side of the distributor below the cap. Pull this hose off and stick a pen, a pencil or a golf tee into the end of it. This is a vacuum hose and to leave it connected would give a false timing indication.

Now start the car and let it warm up for a few minutes. While the car is still idling, come back around to the front and point the timing light at the marks you made on the timing scale and pointer. *Again, be careful of the fan belts and blade.* Because the timing light is a stroboscopic (strobe) light, it very quickly blinks on and off as the Number One plug is fired. When it blinks on the marks you made, it "freezes" them and shows whether both are perfectly aligned. If they are aligned, the ignition timing is O.K. If they are not aligned, the ignition timing must be reset. Make a mental note whether the mark on the scale is before or after the mark on the pointer and then turn the car off.

Underneath the distributor you will find a clamp or bolt which holds the distributor in place in the engine. Loosen that bolt but do not remove it. Restart the engine and let it idle. Aim the timing light at the scale and pointer again and then rotate the whole distributor in its hole to the right or left until the two marks align. When the mark on the scale aligns with the mark on the pointer, shut the car off and tighten the distributor bolt. Recheck the alignment with the engine running and if it was not altered by tightening the distributor, shut the car off, remove the timing light wires and reconnect the Number One spark plug cable.

17. *Clean And Adjust The Carburetor.* The adjustments which must be made on the carburetor include the speed at which the engine idles, the ratio of air to gasoline which enters the

cylinders (commonly known as the mixture), and the proper operation of the automatic choke.

Before making these adjustments, however, it is necessary to clean out the inside passages of the carburetor as well as possible so that dirt particles won't interfere with its operation. Remove the air cleaner if you did not already have to do so to gain access to the distributor. Take a good look at the carburetor and don't let all those hoses, screws and pieces of linkage diminish your resolve.

As you will recall from the earlier discussion, the main function of the carburetor is to mix the air and gasoline in the correct proportion before it goes into the cylinders to be burned. This alone would be an easy enough task but it is made more complex because the proportion must change for varying conditions. When the car is started on a cold morning, for example, this mixture must be richer (a higher proportion of gasoline). For other driving or idling conditions such as warm weather, acceleration, deceleration, full power and idling, the carburetor must supply different ratios of gasoline to air for proper combustion in the cylinders. It accomplishes all these jobs by carefully metering the flow of gasoline and air through many small passages,

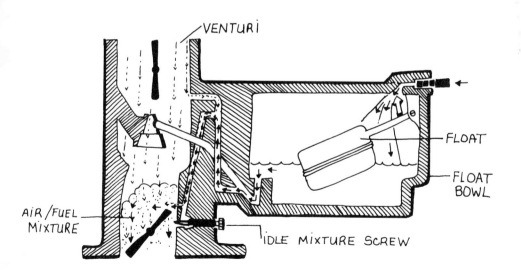

A simplified carburetor and how it works.

valves and nozzles. You can therefore see why the cleanliness of these passages, valves and nozzles is critical. One aid to the internal cleanliness of the carburetor is the gasoline itself which, as you know, is a good cleaning solvent. However, the passage of time and miles and the possibility of impurities in the gas itself can leave gummy, dirty deposits inside the carburetor which will eventually restrict its performance. Cleaning the carburetor externally with a spray solvent should not have to be done more often than every 20,000–25,000 miles and it is often advisable to have the carburetor removed and "rebuilt" (disassembled, cleaned thoroughly and perishable parts replaced) after 50,000–60,000 miles.

Carburetor rebuilding is a job best left to a professional or a serious hobbyist so I am not including it in this book. I will, however, tell how to give it a minor cleaning by spraying some solvent in from the outside of the carburetor.

How a carburetor performs throughout its whole range of tasks is based on how it functions at idle. Once it idles smoothly and at the proper speed, adjusting its performance at other levels will be easier and more accurate.

18. *Adjusting The Idle Mixture.*   Once you have determined whether your car has a one barrel, a two barrel or a four barrel carburetor by looking in the owner's manual or by looking way down inside the carburetor itself and counting the "throats" or round passages at the bottom (they will be about the size of a quarter), find the idle mixture screw(s). The idle mixture screw(s) will be located near the base of the carburetor and usually at the front. If yours is a late model car (1969 or newer) these screws will be covered with a colored plastic cap called a limiter cap. These are present so no one will try to adjust the idle mixture and therefore alter the idle setting phase of the car's emission control system. In fact, it is against the law for commercial service facilities to remove these caps. There is no law against the consumer/owner removing them but if your car has these caps, it is probably better not to tamper with them.

If your car does not have idle limiter caps, locate the idle mixture screw(s) and then start the engine. While it is idling, slowly and carefully remove these screws (if yours is a one barrel carburetor, there will only be one screw). A spring will come out with the screw so be sure you keep track of it. Spray the screw and the spring with solvent and place it on a clean piece of paper to dry. With the engine still idling, direct the solvent spray into each mixture screw hole—about fifteen seconds will do.

Now replace the screws to about halfway in and, if there is only one, screw it in until the engine begins to chug; then back it out about one-half of a turn which should provide the smoothest idle. If your car has two mixture screws, do this same procedure one screw at a time until you attain the smoothest possible idle—identified by your ear. The smoothest idle isn't necessarily the fastest or slowest idle—rather it is the most even. If the idle speed which sounds smoothest to you also sounds too fast or slow to you, don't worry because the idle speed is the next adjustment you will make.

On the right side of the carburetor (as you face it from the front) is the linkage. It is called this because it "links" control of the carburetor to the gas pedal inside the car. If you move this linkage back and forth, it is the same as pumping the gas pedal up and down. Mounted in this linkage you will find an idle speed adjusting screw which sets the limit that the linkage can snap back to when you take your foot off the gas pedal. As you will notice, the linkage works against a spring so that as you press down on the gas pedal, you stretch the spring. When you remove your foot from the pedal, the spring contracts and snaps the linkage back to the minimum, or idle, speed. Exactly where that minimum speed is can be set by adjusting the idle speed screw in and out.

If the engine is idling too fast, adjust its speed with this screw. If the engine is idling so slow that it is barely running or if it can't keep running and stalls, increase the idle speed by adjusting the idle speed screw in or out until a satisfactory idle speed is obtained. If adjusting it "by ear," a satisfactory idle speed should be on the low side—just fast enough to let the engine run smoothly and keep from stalling.

Automatic Chokes

Almost all new American cars come equipped with an automatic choke. This device makes the mixture richer and increases the idle speed when you start a cold engine. Then, as the engine warms up, the mixture becomes less rich (or "leaner") and the idle speed drops back to normal. If your car continually stalls and runs roughly until it warms up, the automatic choke probably needs to be adjusted. Adjusting the choke is complicated and there are too many different types of chokes on today's cars to give you a standard adjustment procedure. However, you can recognize the symptoms of a malfunctioning choke so that you know what to have adjusted by a mechanic.

You have now completed the do-it-yourself tune-up but before putting your tools away and replacing the air cleaner, make a few quick checks of the car's other systems. Check the brake fluid level, the battery water level, the radiator water level, the engine oil level and the transmission fluid level.

Washing, Waxing, and Cleaning

I think this topic is important because I have been in lots of cars that make me feel like getting out and taking a bath.

A dirty car really is unnecessary. A car is like your home or even like your own body: we all spend time maintaining our homes and ourselves in order to look nice, perform better and last longer. It's not surprising that your car requires the same maintenance and for the same reasons. So, keep it clean if only to provide yourself with a pleasant environment and make the car as attractive as possible for resale or trade-in.

A spring cleaning is especially appropriate for cars, they have picked up dirt and salt from winter driving. Any good car soap is preferable to a detergent because the car soap does not remove wax as the detergent will. A bucket of warm, soapy water, a soft sponge and a garden hose is all the equipment you will need.

Wet the car completely and then wash it with the soapy water, a section at a time so the soap won't start to dry on the car, and rinse it off each time. If your car is especially dirty, do this twice—a second wash and rinse will remove all the dirt and film missed on the first wash. If you let the car dry in the sun, the water droplets will dry and leave spots all over the car so it is a good idea to dry them off with a chamois cloth, paper towels or a couple of clean old turkish towels.

Use some window cleaning solvent on both the inside and outside of the windshield and the other windows and dry them with paper towels for the best results—don't forget to do all the mirrors in this manner also.

Waxing

If your car is fairly new and the paint is in good condition, you should wax it once or twice a year and you can use one of the non-buffing type car waxes. Try to wax the car in your garage or in the shade where the hot sun won't get on it. Wax the car a section at a time—one fender, then the hood, then the other fender, then a door, etc. Rub the wax on well, let it dry for a few minutes, and then go back and buff it. You may not believe the difference but your car certainly will—a good coat of wax will do wonders toward making the car look better, making the paint last longer and warding off rust and small nicks.

If your car has not been waxed in a long while and the paint is old and dull, you should "compound" it before giving it a good waxing. Rubbing compound is a slightly abrasive cleaner and it

does its job by rubbing off the gound-in dirt and getting down to the cleaner paint. Because it is fairly strong, don't rub too hard with it. Apply it and buff it out the same way you do with wax—a section at a time and with clean, soft rags. But, keep in mind that after compounding a car's finish you have exposed the surface paint to the elements without the benefit of a protective coat of wax. So right after compounding the car you must also wax it. Because you will then be waxing an unprotected surface it is better to use a paste buffing wax—applied in the same way: a section at a time and then buff with a soft rag.

The chrome bumpers and trim on your car should be polished with some chrome polish made especially for this job. I'm sure you have seen cars with rusty bumpers and trim. Well, chrome parts will last indefinitely if they are protected. Chrome polish is liquid and easy to apply and buff. Just rub it on (underneath too), let it dry and buff it off. Your car will look 100% better and the chrome parts will last forever.

If your car has a vinyl top, there are special cleaners available which will clean and renew it and they are pretty easy to apply. Be sure, however, to do this job in the shade.

There are also special cleaners on the market for tires and whitewalls and they do a good job although they probably aren't much of an improvement over a stiff brush and some heavy-duty powdered cleanser.

Cleaning the Interior

Thoroughly cleaning the inside of your car can make it feel like a new car and look like one too. Again, there are specialized cleaners on the market for automotive interiors but a good home spray type cleaner will surely do just as well. Clean the headliner (ceiling) and sun visors first for they collect a surprising amount of dirt and film, especially if you smoke in the car. Next, clean the top of the dashboard, the instrument panel, the shelf behind the back seat, the door panels, the steering column and finally the seats (if they are vinyl or leather) with this same spray cleaner. Then do the chrome trim on the dash and around the windows with the same chrome polish used on the exterior of the car.

Cleaning the leather or vinyl seats will leave them looking flat and dull but applying a small amount of home furniture (spray) polish with a soft cloth will make them look nicer and protect them from dirt and scratches. This spray polish will also keep dust from sticking on the top of the dashboard. All that remains is to vacuum the rugs and ash trays and wash the floor mats and even a long neglected car will take a new lease on life.

Chapter 8

Watch Out for the Ripoff

It hardly needs to be restated that women have traditionally been a prime target for the automotive con job. Machinery, and the automobile in particular, has for so long been such a strictly male-oriented field and women, due either to lack of interest, time or education, have never established their knowledge of it so we have become easy victim material. I have heard so many cases of women being sold new engines and transmissions for practically new cars that I have concluded that there are two main reasons for this. Either women really haven't taken basic care of the car and the repairs and replacements are legitimate *or* some unscrupulous mechanic is taking advantage of their lack of familiarity with things automotive. If you have read this book and learned about how a car works and how to take care of it, you can now avoid high costs and premature repairs.

You will also know enough about your car and its possible ills to avoid being taken by the unscrupulous mechanic who tries to sell you a repair that your car doesn't need. However, marching into a garage with a chip on your shoulder and proclaiming that you now know all the automotive mysteries and can't be cheated is enough of a challenge that even the marginally honest mechanic might not be able to pass up the opportunity to get the best of you.

Keeping in mind that you still have a lot to learn and that practical experience is probably the best automotive teacher, I think the smartest approach is to keep a low profile for a while.

Mechanic Psychology

When dealing with mechanics and repair garages, it must be established right away that you are not a sucker yet it must be done in such a way that you don't immediately challenge the worst in a man: to prove his superiority over women.

Don't get taken for auto repairs just because you're a woman.

If you bring in a car that is dirty and visibly uncared for or one in which the oil is black and gooey because it has not been changed for 12,000 miles, then right away you have told the mechanic that you don't care and probably don't know anything about your automotive investment. That's the first giveaway. The second strike against you is when he calls to tell you that the car is idling too slowly because five pistons need to be replaced and you believe him. Strike three is when you don't ask how much it will cost. When you pick up the car and get a bill for $400, screaming and yelling will be like arguing with the umpire: futile.

When you take your car in for service, write down *exactly* what you want done and ask the mechanic *exactly* how much it will cost. If you take your car in for repairs and don't know just what is wrong with it, tell him to call you with his discoveries and the cost *before* beginning to fix it. If his diagnosis sounds wrong or too costly to you, tell him not to do it and take the car elsewhere or go see it and have him show you the problem. However, don't

Get a written estimate.

confuse a mistaken diagnosis with a ripoff because mechanics are human and can make honest mistakes. Several studies have been made where a car was prepared with a defect and taken to a dozen garages. Usually the experiment turns up ten different con- clusions. The presumption is that the very expensive ones are ripoffs and the inexpensive ones are mistakes.

Naturally, inexpensive mistakes don't solve the car's original problem but they permit you to give the mechanic the opportuni- ty to rectify the error before you brand him as a cheat and tell all your friends and neighbors not to patronize his garage.

Positive Approach

If you take your car to a garage for service or for diagnosis of a problem, let them know that you are not an easy mark by having a clean, well-maintained car and by conducting business in a positive manner. If the mechanic sees that you value your investment and take care of it and if you give him a written list of the service you want performed or the symptoms of the problem you want him to pinpoint and if you ask him for an on the spot estimate or a telephone call, then he will be much less apt to try to pull a fast one on you. In other words, if you are living proof of the woman driver image, you are inviting the ripoff. But if you take an informed and strictly business attitude, the odds are with you.

You are more apt to be taken while traveling for the simple reason that the mechanic knows he won't be seeing you again and you won't be telling your friends and neighbors in his area what he did to you. In the auto repair business word-of-mouth is the best form of advertising—whether the advertising is positive or negative.

If you do feel that you were taken while traveling, take the time to write to the Better Business Bureau or Chamber of Commerce in that area. Give complete details so that they can give you an honest investigation of the charge. It is very easy to be taken by a garage because most people have very limited knowledge of how a car operates (and they get more complicated every year) which is, again, the reason for this book.

Keep in mind that even though a professional mechanic is very familiar with the automobile he often is searching for a tiny problem among the 15,000 or more parts of the average auto. In addition, the emission systems on modern cars makes his job quite a bit harder . . . so you be fair with him. If he makes a repair and you still have a problem, give him another chance to make good. Then if he doesn't come through, you are justified in shouting to the world what a louse he is and telling him that you do not intend to return to his garage and that you plan to tell your friends about him.

Garages build their repair business on good will so anyone who cares about their business should also be willing to promote good will by giving good, honest, fairly priced service. So this is your most effective lever against crooked garages. By spreading the word to his potential customers and by complaining to the Better Business Bureau, Chamber of Commerce and any local business groups, you hit the dishonest shop where it hurts—in the reputation.

Needless to say, such treatment should be reserved only for the real thing because helping to put an honest shop out of business on the basis of an error in judgment, a petty price disagreement or a genuine mistake would be a miserable thing to be responsible for.

Knowing for sure whether you have been cheated is often very difficult unless the garage did some job on your car which you didn't authorize or unless their charge for a job is out of all proportion with the going rate for that same job in other shops. The difficult task for you is knowing whether or not a particular job was really necessary, whether it was in fact done and whether it was done well. Some people will recommend that you ask to see the worn parts or ask to have them after the new ones are installed. But would you know a worn piston from an new one? Probably not. Piston wear is measured in thousandths of inches—obviously not visible to the eye. In fact, there are many, many automotive parts whose condition cannot be easily defined. Points, spark plugs, brake linings, tires, hoses and fan belts visibly show their condition but, of course, these parts are the ones most likely to wear out and they are usually the cheapest to replace. Unless such components have been recently replaced, the chances are good that when a mechanic tells you they are worn—they are.

The most ideal areas for cheating women car owners are the exotic jobs such as transmission work, internal engine work, front end and suspension repairs. Any parts that are not normally in view or whose worn appearance is not visibly different from their normal appearance are repair or replacement jobs that you should be wary of. In addition, any job that is unusually expensive should arouse your suspicion. I realize that "unusually expensive" is a rather vague term so this chapter provides a chart showing how long parts should last, what is most likely to go wrong with them and why, and how their life can be lengthened if possible.

A word of caution, however; any chart-like presentation of facts gives the impression of being gospel whereas there are always exceptions to any rules. Your best guide here is to keep an open mind and not be too dogmatic. Also remember that costs of parts and labor are constantly rising so just beware of the dramatic price difference.

By necessity, this chart only lists the cost of replacement parts whether new or rebuilt. To these must be added the cost of labor and that will vary from shop to shop at $6.00 to $14.00 per hour. I know from personal experience that the cost of good mechanical ability and training is high. There are not enough automotive mechanics to go around and the highly qualified ones are expensive. Garage owners are willing to pay for them, however, because they know their job well, satisfy the customers and work fast. But the cost of a highly skilled mechanic is passed on to the customer as in any other business.

The accompanying chart is intended to give a smattering of prices for whole jobs. Naturally, these prices are average and will vary somewhat from car to car. Furthermore, these prices are generally for whole jobs whereas often an individual component can be repaired, rebuilt or replaced for much less. For example, an automatic transmission may cost $500.00 to completely replace while an individual gear or bearing may cost $25.00.

Remember, there are 15,000 or more parts in every automobile so to list them all would be impossible. Equally impossible is the task of stating how long each component will last. It is not unusual for parts that should last for the life of the car to break after 10,000 miles due to some freak defect. Conversely, parts which are supposed to last for 10,000 miles have been known to hang on for 75,000 miles. So, the life expectancies I have listed are averages and often minimums.

In scanning the chart you will notice how many parts should last for the life of the car. This is not unusual for any machinery will last a long time with proper care. The more sophisticated the machine (such as an automobile) the more necessary is proper maintenance.

Component Analysis Chart

	Life Expectancy	Replacement or Repair Cost	How & Why	Prevention
Air Cleaner	1 yr./12,000 miles	$4.00	Fills up w/dirt	None
Air Conditioner	Should last for life of car but drive belt & hoses may deteriorate	$25.00	Wear, lack of maintenance	Annual inspection, lubrication
Air Conditioning Tune	1 yr./12,000 miles	$15–25.00	Normal wear	None
Alternator	Life of car but drive belt 15–25,000 miles	$80.00	Old age or hard wear	None
		$3.00 belt		None
Automatic Transmission	Life of car w/fluid changes every 35,000 miles	$300–600.00	Abuse	Change fluid and adjust when necessary
Axle, Rear & Differential	Life of car but check oil w/every oil change	$150.00	Abuse	Check oil level
Battery	2–4 years	$20.–40.00	Age and deterioration	Check level and clean terminals regularly.
Battery Cables	2–4 years	$7.00 both	Corrosion	Clean & coat w/grease
Bearings, Engine	Life of car	$50–75.00	Extremely hard wear & no oil changes	Change oil regularly
Bearings, Wheel	Life of car	$20.–25. (4)	Hard wear & lack of grease	Keep packed w/grease
Brakes				
Master Cylinder	Life of car but check fluid regularly	$30.00	Wear or age	———
Wheel Cylinders	30–40,000 miles	$30.00 (4)	Wear	None

Part	Life Expectancy	Cost	Cause	Prevention
Shoes (linings)	15–30,000 miles	$40.00 (4)	Wear	None
Drums	Life of car	$50.00 (4)	Scoring by worn brake shoes	Replace bad shoes in time
Disc Pads	15–30,000 miles	$60.00 (4 sets)	Wear	None
Rotor	Life of car	$35.00 each	Scoring by worn pads	Replace worn pads in time
Cables, Ignition	Minimum 25,000 miles	$10.00	Age	None
Carburetors	Life of car but over-haul may be necessary every 30–50,000 miles	$30–80.00 (new) $10–25.00 (overhaul)	Wear of internal parts	None
Clutch Assembly	Should last at least 40,000 miles unless abused	$40.00	Wear caused by riding the clutch pedal	Shift properly; don't ride pedal
Coil	Life of car	$10.00	Normal wear	None
Condenser	1 yr/12,000 miles	$1.00	Normal wear	None
Connecting Rods	Life of car	$10.00 each	Abuse	Regular oil changes
Cooling System Tune-Up	1 yr./12,000 miles	$15.00	Age, Leaks	——
Crankshaft	Life of car	$100.00	Abuse	Regular oil changes
Cylinder Head & Valve System	Life of car	$65.00 each—Head $6.00 each—Valves	Hard wear, old age or abuse	Regular oil changes and tune-ups
Differential	Life of car	$75.00	Abuse	Check lubrication regularly
Distributor	Life of car	$30.00	Faulty part or very hard wear	None
Door Windows	Life of car	$30.00	Accident	None

Component Analysis Chart—*continued*

	Life Expectancy	Replacement or Repair Cost	How & Why	Prevention
Door Locks	Life of car	$10.00	Rust or damage	Occasional lubrication
Driveshaft	Life of car	$25.00	Damage	None
Emission Control System Tune-Up	1 yr./12,000 miles	$15.00	Normal wear	None
Engine Block	Life of car	$200–600.00	Abuse or damage	Regular oil changes
Engine Mounts	Life of car	$15.00	Damage	None
Engine Oiling System	Life of car except filter	$25.00	Abuse	Regular oil changes
Exhaust Manifolds	Life of car	$20.00 each	Damage, very hard wear	None
Exhaust Pipes	50,000 miles	$20.00 per side	Heat, wear & rust	None
Fan Belts	15–20,000 miles	$3.00 each	Normal wear	None
Filter, Oil	3,000 miles	$2.00	Fills w/impurities	None
Flywheel	Life of car	$40.00	Damage	None
Front End Alignment	25,000 miles unless badly jolted	$15.00	Potholes, curbs, wear	
Fuel Pump	50,000 miles	$15.00	Age & wear	None
Fuel Tank	Life of car	$35–50.00	Damage	None
Hand Brake	Life of car unless frozen	$15.00	Freezing	Lubrication; don't use in extremely cold weather

Part	Interval/Life	Cause	Cost	Maintenance
Headlights	25,000 miles	Age	$3.00	None
Heater	Life of car	Rust, age	$20.00 Core	None
		Wear, age	$35.00 Blower	
Horn	Life of car	Damage	$8.00	None
Ignition Switch	Life of car	Faulty parts	$3.00	None
Intake Manifolds	Life of car	Damage	$50.00	None
Muffler	40,000 miles	Heat wear & rust	$15–20.00	None
Oil Pump	Life of car	Abuse, hard wear	$20.00	Regular oil changes
Parking Lights	Bulbs—3 yrs.	Age or breakage	$.50—bulbs	None
			$2.00—lens	
PCV Valve	2 yrs./25,000 miles	Wear	$2.00	Clean in solvent at every tune-up
Pistons	Life of car	Abuse, hard wear	$8.00 each	Regular oil changes
Rings, pins	Life of car	Abuse, hard wear	$6.00 per piston set	Regular oil changes
Points	1 yr./12,000 miles	Age & wear	$4.00	None
Power Steering				
Belt	15,000 miles	Age & wear	$3.00	None
Pump	Life of car	Age & wear	$30–50.00	Maintain fluid level
Radiator	Life of car	Damage	$80.00 (new)	Annual flushing
Cap	50,000 miles	Leaks	$15.00 (recore)	None
Hoses	25,000 miles	Wear	$2.00	None
		Age & wear	$6.00 (both)	None

Component Analysis Chart—*continued*

	Life Expectancy	Replacement or Repair Cost	How & Why	Prevention
Shock Absorbers	35,000 miles	$10.00 each	Wear	None
Spark Plugs	1 yr./12,000 miles	$1.20 each	Normal wear & age	None
Springs	Life of car	$35.00 each	Wear	None
Standard Transmissions	Life of car	$300–500.00	Abuse	Maintain fluid level
Starter	50,000 miles	$40–70.00 (new)	Age & wear	None
Taillights	2 yrs.—bulbs	$ .50—bulb $5.00—lens	Age or damage	None
Thermostat	3 yrs.	$3.00	Deterioration	None
Tires	15,000–50,000 miles depending on type & use			
Tune-Up	1 yr./12,000 miles	$15–65.00 each $12–35.00 including labor	Wear Normal Age & wear	None None
Universal Joints	50,000 miles	$8.00 each	Wear	None
Water Pump	50,000 miles	$25.00	Age & wear	Occasional lubrication
Wheels	Life of car	$20.00 each	Damage	None
Windshields	Life of car	$100.00	Damage	None
Windshield Wiper Assy.	Life of car	$45.00	Age or damage	None
Blades	15–25,000 miles	$5.00	Normal age & wear	None

Diagnostic Centers

A relatively new part of the automotive service business is the diagnostic center and it can be very helpful to the consumer as well as the do-it-yourselfer. The purpose of a diagnostic center is to find any problems in a car. This is done by attaching the car's systems to a sophisticated computer-like analyzing machine and reading the test results. These machines can accurately measure the state of tune of the engine and its systems and tell the owner

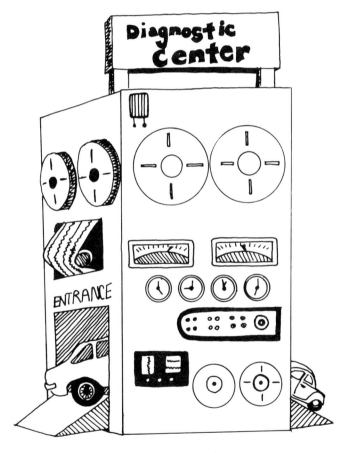

just what repairs or adjustments are required. Where the diagnostic centers have fallen short is their tie-in with repair garages who use them to create business for themselves. As you can guess, the diagnostic machines can be made to tell what the operator wishes them to tell. In unethical hands the diagnostic center becomes simply a sales tool to drum up work (real or phony) for the affiliated repair garage.

However, diagnostic centers can be useful. If you bring your car to one and make it clear that you simply want a test and do not intend to have work done, then chances are good that you will receive a fair and realistic analysis of your car's current condition. The diagnostic center can also be useful to double check the need for repair suggestions that you suspect may not be needed. But, again, make it clear to the operator that you do not intend to have any work done.

For the potential do-it-yourselfer who has not yet developed an experienced eye, the diagnostic center can accomplish most of her troubleshooting work and point out just where replacements and adjustments are needed.

How To Choose A Garage

For the car owner, particularly the one who does not do her own repair and tune-up work, choosing the proper garage is extremely important. Much peace of mind as well as protection of

pocketbook can result from knowing that your car is in the hands of a competent, honest and trustworthy mechanic. But how do you find such a person?

The most valuable recommendations are those which come from your friends who are satisfied customers of a particular garage. If a customer is dissatisfied with a garage's service, she will be its loudest detractor. However, satisfied customers usually have little to say about how good a certain garage is because they expect it to be good. So, if you hear a good recommendation, the garage must have done something very good to warrant it. Personal recommendations based on actual experience rather than hearsay should yield the best results. Don't hesitate to tell the new garage owner who recommended him to you so that you establish an immediate relationship. As in most other areas, you will get the best service and price from a friend.

Another method of evaluating a garage is by trying it yourself for routine maintenance and see how their service and prices are. It may take a bit longer to develop a relationship or to judge their competence and honesty but the results will be the same.

When checking out a garage yourself look for cleanliness, operating efficiency, mechanics who aren't complaining all the time, modern tools and equipment and a willingness to freely discuss prices and repairs and explain them to you. You will probably wonder why a garage, of all places, should be clean. Well, my experience has shown that a garage which cares about keeping the place clean and tidy also cares about doing a good, clean job on your car. Likewise, the garage which is run efficiently will also do efficient repair work and the employees who like their shop and care about its reputation will take more care with your car. Of course, modern tools and equipment show a commitment to the latest trade developments and to building a bigger and better business. Last but not least, an open approach to prices and a willingness to explain and show the job to customers indicate that this garage is a responsible member of the business community and not trying to hide their prices for any unethical reason. On a less specific level, the quality of communication between you and the garage mechanic will be determinant of how well you can do business together. Half of the responsibility for developing this level of communication is yours and hopeful this book has prepared you to do so.

Personal Car Data

Car Dealer _____ Tel. _____

Make _____ Year _____

Model _____ Body Style _____

Title Number _____

Registration Number _____

Manufacturer's Serial Number _____

License Number _____

Driver's License Number _____

_____

Insurance Company _____

Agent _____

Policy Number _____

Engine (Displacement & no. of cylinders) _____

Transmission _____

Spark Plug Size & Gap _____

Tire Size _____

Tire Pressure _____

Engine Oil Capacity _____ quarts

Gas Tank Capacity _____ gallons

Distributor Point Gap _____ in. Dwell _____ °

Ignition Timing _____ °

Index

Numbers set in **boldface** indicate illustrations

Acceleration, 7
Accelerator, 7
Accelerator pump, 7
Accessories, 7
Accidents, 77-79
    avoidance of, 79
    and insurance, 78
Acid, 7; See also Corrosion
Advance, 7
Aerial, 7
Air cleaner, 7
    and filter, **100**
    See also Component Analysis Chart,
        Fuel System
Air conditioning, 7, 186
    compressor, 13
    problem areas, 121, 122
    tune-up, 186
Air-fuel ratio, 8
Air pump, 8
Alignment and chassis lubrication,
    152
Alternator, 8
    description and purpose, 97
    light, 91
    See also Component Analysis Chart
Ammeter, 8

Amperes (amps), 8
Analyzer, 8
Antifreeze, 8, 74; See also Radiator
Armature, 8
Automatic transmission, 8
    fluid, 8, 113
    See also Component Analysis Chart
Axle, 8; See also Component Analysis
    Chart

Backfire, 9
Backingplate, 9
Backup lights, 9
Bakelite, 9
Balancing, 9
Barrel, 9
Battery, 9, **99**; See also Component
    Analysis Chart
    acid, 9
    booster, 9
    cables, 9; See also Component
        Analysis Chart
    cells, 9
    charging, 9, 91
    corrosion, elimination of, 135
    level, maintenance of, 127
    life, 75

location and identification of, **99**
and starting, 148
water, 75
Bearings, 10
  engine, Component Analysis Chart
  wheel, Component Analysis Chart
Belted tires, 10; *See also* Tires
Bias-ply, 10; *See also* Tires
Bleeding, 10
Block, 10
Blow-by, 10
Blower motor, 10
Body, 10
Bolts, 10
Bore and stroke, 10; *See also* Engine
Brakes, 10; *See also* Component
    Analysis Chart
  causes for squeaking, 156
  description of system, **105,** 106,
    107, 108
  disc, 108
  disc pads, Component Analysis
    Chart
  drum, 9, 10, 106; *See also*
    Component Analysis Chart
  fluid, 105, 106
  freezing of, 76
  lights, 10, 136
  lines, 10
  linings, 106
  master cylinder, Component
    Analysis Chart, 22
  power, 10
  rotor, Component Analysis Chart
  self-adjusting, 10, 26
  troubleshooting, 106
  and water, 72
  wheel cylinder, Component
    Analysis Chart
Breakdown, 162
  avoidance of (checklist), 88
  procedures, 79-80
Breaker points, 11; *See also* Ignition
Breather, 11
Bucket seats, 11
Bumpers, 11
Bushing, 11
Buying, 34
  considerations, 34
  driving habits, 39
  large cars, 34
  personal considerations, 37-39

Cable, 11
Cables, ignition, Component Analysis
    Chart
  installation of, 171
Camber, 11; *See also* Alignment
Camshaft, 11
Cancer, 11, 141-142
Capacity, 11
Carbon, 11
Carbon monoxide, 12, 118
  warning, 45
Carburetor, 12; *See also* Component
    Analysis Chart
  additives, 76
  adjusting and cleaning, 172-174
  location and function of, 100, **101**
Caster, 12
Chassis, 12
Chatter, 12; *See also* Clutch
Children, and locked cars, 62
Choke, 12
  automatic, 175, 176
Circuit, 12; *See also* Electrical
    system
Cleaning, interior, 178-179
Clearance, 12; *See also* Cylinder
Clutch, 85-88; *See also* Component
    Analysis Chart
Coil, 12; *See also* Electrical system
Combustion, 12, 117
  chamber, 12
  See also Cylinder, Fuel system
Components, 12; *See also* Parts
Component Analysis Chart, 186-190
Compression, 12
  gauge, 13
Compressor, 13; *See also* Air
    conditioning
Condensation, 13
Condenser, 166-167; *See also*
    Component Analysis Chart
Conductor, 13
Connecting Rods, 13; *See also*
    Component Analysis Chart
Console, 13
Coolant, 13
Cooling, 73-74
Cooling system, **111,** 125, 126
  components described, 109-110
  tune-up, Component Analysis Chart
Cornering, 13
Corrosion, 13

Cotter pin, 13
Crankcase, 13; *See also* Engine block
  blow-by, 10
Cranking, 14; *See also* Starting
Crankshaft, 14; *See also* Component
    Analysis Chart
Cupping, 14; *See also* Tire
Current, 14
Cycle, 14; *See also* Pistons
Cylinder, 12, 13, 14; *See also*
    Component Analysis Chart

Dashboard, 14, **90,** 91, 92
  lights, testing and replacement, 139
Defroster, 14
Depreciation, 50
Detonation, 14; *See also* Knock
Diagnose, 14
Diagnostic centers, 191-192
Dieseling, 14
  cure for, 155
Differential, 14, 116-117, Component
    Analysis Chart; *See also* Axle
Dimmer, 14
Dipstick, 15; *See also* Oil system,
    Automatic transmission
Direct current (DC), 15
Discharge, 15; *See also* Battery
Displacement, 15
Distributor, 15, **166,** 167-170,
    Component Analysis Chart
  cables, 15
  cam
    lubrication of, 167-168
    rotation of, 169-170
  cap, 15
  and electrical system, 149
  rotor, 15
  See also Ignition system
Door locks and windows, Component
    Analysis Chart
Downshift, 86-87
Drain pan, 158
Driving
  and drinking, 56-57
  and drugs, 56-57
  techniques, 55-56
Drivebelt, 112
Driveshaft, 15, 116-117; *See also*
    Component Analysis Chart
Drivetrain, components of, 116
Drum, 15; *See also* Brakes

Dwell angle, 15
Dwell meter, 15
  and points gap, 170-171

Electrical system, 15
Electricity, and the starting
    mechanism, 148-149
Electrode, 15
  and spark plugs, 149
Electrolyte, 15
Emergency lights, 139-140
Emission control, 120-121
  system, 8, 15
  tune-up, Component Analysis
    Chart
Engine, air cooled, 8; *See also*
    Component Analysis Chart
  block, 10
  crankcase, 13
  cylinder operation diagram, 103
  cylinders, 14
  diesel, 14
  four-cylinder, 94
  mounts, 16, 96
  oil, 123
  six-cylinder, 95
  types described, 92
  V-eight, **96**
Equipment; *See* Tools
Ethyl gasoline, 16
Estimates, tips on, 182-183
Evaporation, 16
Exhaust, 16; *See also* Component
    Analysis Chart
  manifold, 16
  noise, 154
  problems, 118-119
  system, 117-118

Fading, 16; *See also* Brakes
Fan, 16
Fan belts, 16, 96, **97,** 98, 130
  function of, 98
  squeak, 155
Fatigue, 16
Feathering, 16; *See also* Tires
Feeler gauge, 16
Fire extinguisher, **43**
  treatment, 131
Firewall, 16
Firing order, 17
Fishtailing, 17

Flares, **41,** 42
Flashers, 17
Flashlights, 42
Float bowl, 17; *See also* Carburetor
Flooding, 17
Floorboard, 17
Fluid, 17
Fouling, 17; *See also* Spark plugs
Four-speed transmission, 84-88
Frame, 17
Freon, 17
Friction, 17
Front Suspension, 17; *See also* Steering
Fuel, 17
   injection, 17
   nozzle, 18
   problems
      and carburetor, 147-148
      and vaporlock, 148
   pump, 18
      location of, **101**
      maintenance of, 148
   system, 18
   tank, 18
Fumes, 18
Fuse, 18
   location and replacement of
      138-139

Garages
   advantages of, 45
   choice of, 192-193
   See also Mechanics
Gas gauge, 91-92
Gasket, 18
Gasoline, 18
Gas pedal; *See* Accelerator
Gas tank, 119
Gauges, 18, 91
Gear ratio, 18
   shift, 18
   shift patterns, 84-85
Generator, 18; *See also* Alternator
Grabbing, 18; *See also* Brakes
Grab point, 85
Ground, 18

Hammer, 42, 43
Handbrake, 19
Hazard lights, 60
Headlights, 19, 140
Heater, 19
Hitchhikers, **61**

Hood, 19
Horn, 19
Horsepower, 19
Hoses, 19
   air conditioning, 110
   radiator, 110
Hubcap, removal of, **70**
H-shift pattern, **85;** *See also* Gearshift
Hydraulic, 19
   brakes, 19
   valves, 20
Hydrocarbons, 20
Hydrometer, 20; *See also* Battery

Idle, 20, 64
   adjustment, 20
   limiter caps, 20
   mixture, 20
      adjustment of, 174-175
   speed and choke, 175-176
Ignition, 20
   problems, 146-147
   switch, Component Analysis Chart
   system, 20, 101-105, **168**
   timing; *See* Tune-up
   timing procedure, 171-172
   wet wires, 73
In-line engine, 20
Inspection, 47-48
Instruments, 20; *See also* Gauges
Insurance, 77-78
   types of, 48-50
Intake manifold, 20; *See also*
      Component Analysis Chart
Internal combustion engine, 21

Jack, 41, **67**
   use of, 66-69
Jet, 21
Jumper cables, 21, 44
   use of, 151, **152, 153**
Jump starting, 141.

Kerosene, 21
Keys
   tips on, 44
   lost, compensating for, 157
Kickdown switch, 21; *See also* Passing
      gear
Knock, 21; *See also* Detonation

Labor costs, 185
Leaf spring, 21; *See also* Suspension

Leaks, valve cover, 143
Lean mixture, 21; *See also* Carburetor
Limited slip differential, 21
Linings, 21; *See also* Brakes
Loans, 36-37
Locks, 59
  frozen, 157
Lube job, 22
Lubricant, 22
Lubrication, 161
  chassis, 130
  importance of, 63
Lubricating system, 22
Lug nuts, removal of, 22, 69-70
Lug wrench, 41
  use of, **67**

Mags, 22
Maintenance interval chart, 143-144
Manifold, 22
Manufacturers handbook, 45-46; *See also* Owners Manual
Master cylinder, 22; *See also* Brakes
Mechanical failure, and preventive maintenance, 150
Mechanics, 183
Mirrors, use of, **53,** 54
Misalignment, symptoms of, 152
Misfiring, 22
Mixture, 22; *See also* Carburetor
Muffler, 22, 117; *See also* Component Analysis Chart
  noise, 154-155

Negative, 22; *See also* Circuit
Nuts, 22

Octane, 23
Ohm, 23
Oil, 23
  capacity, 23
  changes
    reason and timing, 93-95
    changes, procedure, 158
  dipstick, reading of, **124**
  disposal of, 160
  filter, 23, 158
    workings of, 94-95
  pan, 23
  pressure gauge, 91
  pump; *See also* Component Analysis Chart
  purchase of, 158

system, **97**
  See also Lubricant
Out-of-round, 23
Overdrive, 23
Overheating and antifreeze, 150
  symptons amd problems, 151
Oversteer, 23
Owners manual, 51-52; *See also* Manufacturers' handbook

Parking lights, 23; *See also* Component Analysis Chart
Parking safety, 60
Parts, Life expectancy; *See also* Component Analysis Chart
  purchase of for tune up, 164
PCV (positive crankcase ventilation) valve, 23; *See also* Component Analysis Chart
Petroleum, 23
Ping, 23; *See also* Detonation, Knock
Pistons, 12, 13, 24; *See also* Component Analysis Chart
Play, 24; *See also* Steering
Pliers, **42**
Points, 24; *See also* Component Analysis Chart, Distributor
  description and function, 104-105
  procedure for changing, 166-167
  spacing (gap), 169-170
Pollution, air, 120-121
Positraction, 24; *See also* Limited slip differential
Powersteering, 24; *See also* Component Analysis Chart
  fluid, 127
  squeal, 155-156
Powertrain, 24
Pre-ignition, 24
Pressure, 24
Pressure cap, 24; *See also* Radiator
Preventive maintenance, 81; *See also* Component Analysis Chart
  exhaust system, 117-118
  gas tank, 119
  tire pressure, 128, 130
  transmission, 116-117
Problems, Chapter, 12
  air conditioner, 121-122
  exhaust, 118-119
  fuel, 147-148
  transmission, 156

Pulley, 24
Pulling, 25; *See also* Brakes

Radiator, 8; *See also* Component
    Analysis Chart
  cap, 25
  core, 25
  engine cooling, 25
  flushing, **74**
  hoses, 25
  location and function, 109
  See also Cooling system
Rear, 25
Recall, 25
Registration, 25
  tips, 46
Regulator, 25, 98; *See also* Alternator,
    Electrical system
Repairs; *See* Diagnostic centers,
    Garages
Resistance, 25
Retard, 25; *See also* Timing
Retiring, 131
Revolutions-per-minute (RPM), 25
Rich mixture, 25; *See also* Carburetor
Rim, 25; *See also* Wheel
Road conditions, 64-65
Road surfaces, 64
  and tires, 64
  and weather, 64
Rotor, 26, 166-170; *See also*
    Distributor, Disc brakes
Rotary Engine, 26

Safety, 53-62
  personal protection, 59-60
  tips, 54
Sagging, 26; *See also* Springs
Scewdriver, **42**
Seatbelts, 54, 59
Sealed beam headlights, 26
Seizing, 26; *See also* Oil
Sending gauges, 27
Skidding, 75-76; *See also* Cornering
Sheet metal, 26
Shift; *See* Gearshift
Shift linkage, 26
Shimmy, 26
Shock absorber, 26, 114, **115,** 116;
    See also Component Analysis
    Chart
Shoe, 27; *See also* Brakes
Shopping; *See* Buying

Short circuit, 27
Shroud, 27; *See also* Fan
Slip, 27; *See also* Clutch
Snow, 75
Solenoid, 27
  switch, 146-147
Spare, 27
Spark, 27
Spark knock, 27, 155; *See also* Knock,
    Ping
Spark plugs, 104; *See also* Component
    Analysis Chart, Tune-up
Specifications, 27
Speedometer, 27
Springs, 114-115; *See also* Component
    Analysis Chart
Stalling, 27
Starter, 27; *See also* Component
    Analysis Chart
Starter switch, 28
Starting tips, 58-59, 63-64
Starving, 28
Steering, 28, 112
  cotterpin, 13
Stickshift, 84
Stroke, 28; *See also* Piston
Summerizing, 73-75
Surging, 28; *See also* Carburetor
Suspension, 28
  front and rear, 114
  front-end suspension, purpose for,
    113
Synchromesh, 28

Tachometer, 28
Tailgating, 79
Tail lights, 28; *See also* Component
    Analysis Chart
  replacement of, 136-138
Tailpipe, 28
Tappets, 28
Temperature gauge, 91
Terminal, 28
Terminology, 39-41
Thermometer, 28
Thermostat, 110; *See also* Component
    Analysis Chart
Tolerance, 29
Tire, chocks, 65, **66**
  conversion chart, 133; *See also*
    Component Analysis Chart
  maintenance and troubleshooting
    128-130

pressure, 128-130
removal of, **72**
size numbering system, 131-132
types, 29, 132-134
Throttle, 28
Throw-out bearing, 28; *See also* Clutch
Tie-rod, 28
Timing, 29
light, 29
See also Tune-up
Tools, 41-44
purchase of, 162-163
Torque, 29
Trade-in value, 34-35
Transmission, 29
behavior of, 116-117
function of, 84
noise, 156
reading of fluid level, 124-125
standard, 83-34
Tips, preparation for, 83
Troubleshooting, 29; *See also*
Diagnosis
Tune-up, 29; *See also* Component
Analysis Chart
and air pollution, 121
procedure, 164
and travel, 82
Turn signals, 30
Turning radius, 30

Understeer, 30
Universal Joints, 30
noise, 156
See also Component Analysis Chart,
Drive train

Vacuum, 30
Valves, 30
covers, 30
tap, 154

Valve job, 30
Vapor, 31
Vapor lock, 31
V-eight engine, 31
Velocity, 31
Vibration, 31
Viscosity, 31
Vise, 31
Volume, 31
Voltage, 31
regulator, 75
See also Electrical system
Voltmeter, 31

Wandering, 31
Warm-up, 63-64
Warranty, 31
Washing, 176
Water jackets, 31
Water leaks, 142-143
radiator, 142
water pump, 143
Water pump, 31; *See also*
Component Analysis Chart
location and function, 109
See also Component Analysis Chart
Waxing, 177-178
Weather, 72-76
conditions and roads, 64-65
Wheel balancing, 32, 131
Wheel base, 31
Wheelbearings, 32
Wheel chocks, **41**
Wheels, 31; *See also* Component
Analysis Chart
Windshield, 32
washer, 32
wipers, 32
Winterizing, 73-75
Wrench, 32, **42**

Dorothy Jackson

Better known as Dottie to her friends and customers, was born and raised in West Chester, Pennsylvania. When only sixteen years old, she took a job as a secretary at Yarnall's Garage across the street from her home. Soon she became interested in the shop operations and, by age 18, was becoming proficient in diagnosing and repairing customers' cars. At this point, her mechanical education was accelerated by the shortage of civilian mechanics caused by World War II. After the war, she had learned enough to continue in her capacity as secretary *and* mechanic in the growing repair shop.

For thirty-one years automobiles have been more than a hobby to Ms. Jackson; they have been a job and a way of life. She works nine hours a day, five days a week, still with Yarnall's Garage, and still is very interested in automobiles and their care. In 1973 Ms. Jackson became the first woman to pass the Chester County State Inspection Examination, a difficult test given to professional mechanics by the Pennsylvania State Police.